BEFORE ALL THINGS

BECOMING ROOTED, BUILT UP, AND
ESTABLISHED IN WHAT MATTERS MOST

BEFORE ALL THINGS

BECOMING ROOTED, BUILT UP, AND ESTABLISHED IN WHAT MATTERS MOST

PRESTYN KYLIE COTUNA
WITH
CHRISTIAN COTUNA

#beforeallthingsbook

If you like this read, please tell your friends

Contents

Forward

By Christian Cotuna

When I met Prestyn for the first time, one of the greatest things that stood out to me was her love for God's Word and her desire to write about it in a way that brought it to life. That was wildly attractive to me. She was (and still is) absolutely beautiful, but the thing that stood out about her was her depth which was rooted in her love for Jesus and her courage to talk about Him in any aspect of her life. As a single young man, that was my one request to God in regards to my future wife, "Lord, please help my future wife to build her whole life on you; help her to have such a deep relationship with you that she may have a heart after your own." As a young man who wanted to lead my future wife and family in a way totally open to Christ's plans for us, I knew that a strong wife who had the exact same sole desire in life as I did would be an extreme necessity.

Shortly after I met Prestyn, I stumbled upon her blog where she began writing the first few chapters of what is now "Before All Things" and my heart jumped out of my chest. Here was a young lady who was in an art program at a very secular school in Portland, OR (what I would consider a dark and discouraging environment for any Christian), but she wasn't afraid to incorporate her love of Jesus into her life, use her God given gifts, and share about the beauty of scripture to anybody who came into her life or crossed her social media. Her identity was in Christ, and it was absolutely beautiful.

Long story short, our relationship started out with me simply writing her a letter to acknowledge her amazing God-given gifts and encourage her to never stop using them to glorify God in whatever her future may hold. Little did I know that about a year later, we would be married, and my beautiful wife would be finishing this project that started out as a dream God gave her many years before, and publishing it so that God could bless others through it too!

I share the background of how this book began for two reasons. The first is to encourage each and every one of you to recognize your God-given talents and passions and start using them in any and every way that enters your mind. When Prestyn started, her first blog post reached 17 people...and today God is using those very same words to reach countless more than we would have ever imagined! My God-given passion is using healthcare to bless others physically, emotionally, and spiritually by reflecting Christ in my work. It's totally different than my wife's dreams, but it didn't matter, what was unbelievably attractive to me was to see that the woman I was in a relationship with had the same basic desire in her heart to love and serve people with the same heart Jesus would. Neither of us were (or are) perfect in that, but the DESIRE is there, and that common rootedness of our souls in Jesus is what brings us together no matter what struggles attack our relationships, lives, and dreams.

The second reason is simply to encourage this heart in every relationship you have, especially your spouse. So many people don't see their God-given dreams or gifts on their own—but guess what—God often gives the people that know and love us the most insight to help identify them and encourage them in us. And the greatest key to a successful marriage is to be first and foremost focused and established in your relationship with Jesus. If that is the greatest goal for each of you, no matter what knocks you off your path, you both will always meet again chasing after that same desire to follow Jesus' footsteps and live like He did. Since we've been married, Prestyn and I have had wonderful opportunities, but also an amazingly overwhelming number of stresses. During Prestyn's time of writing this book, we lost a significant portion of our income, and pretty much every available financial security we had, to support the dream of God working through this book. It absolutely wasn't easy, and didn't even make sense many times, but the one thing we could hold onto was that God was undoubtedly wanting Prestyn to finish this book and get it out there for all to read. And through it all, God has more than provided for us, many times at the last minute, but we wouldn't change our past plans for anything knowing that God will be glorified through this book. Having a heart of encouragement even through tough times was no great act. It was, and is, my role as a husband and fellow believer to build up God's kingdom in any way I can...especially at home, but also anywhere in this world. And the result is the greatest sense of peace, the most miraculous of "God stories", and the most greatest blessing you could ever imagine!

So when you see someone using any one of their talents for God's glory, acknowledge it and encourage them to always keep up the good work! And when your boyfriend, or girlfriend, or spouse, or sibling, or best friend doesn't really know in full their dreams, encourage them in their small pursuits of Jesus because you never know how the smallest of acts can be multiplied by God to reach the farthest ends of the world...and there is nothing more life changing or fulfilling than to see God being glorified on earth and to one day hear those words in Heaven, "Well done, good and faithful servant!"

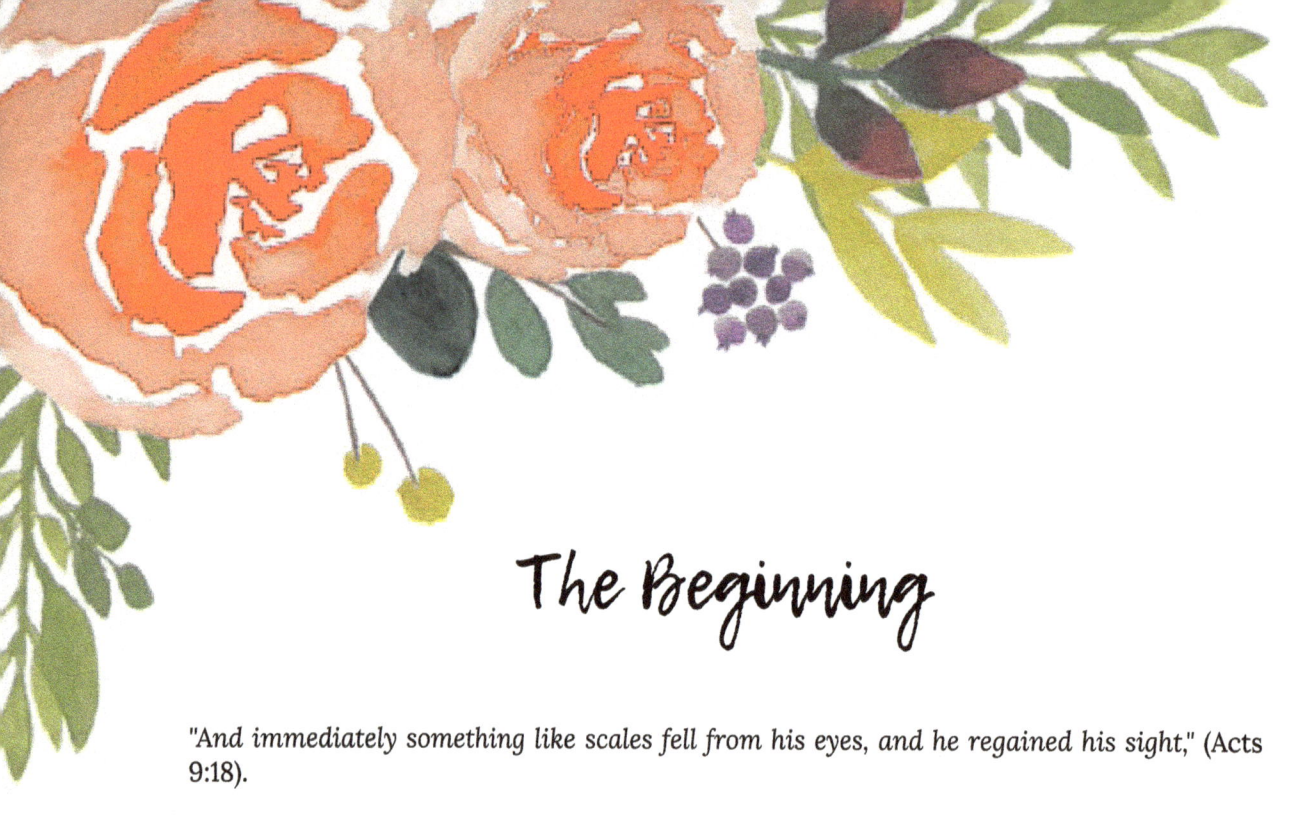

The Beginning

"And immediately something like scales fell from his eyes, and he regained his sight," (Acts 9:18).

Something like scales.

The majority of the time I only see things the way I want to see them. And more often than not, what I'm seeing isn't the whole picture. What would it take for me to see things as they truly are? Probably something like scales would have to fall from my eyes first.

And oh, how they did fall when I turned my attention to Colossians.

Before that, I was a mess. My daily routine was filled with chronic inexplicable pain throughout my body and tearful anxiety attacks at the thought of going to work. The days were gray and rainy and I was so very tired.

Where was God in this? To me, he felt terribly silent. I begged for him to change my situation, and I was terrified of the possibility that he wouldn't. My prayers looked a lot like half-faith: *"Abba, please take my pain away and heal me."* I was too afraid to pray for his will to be done because I couldn't even bear the thought of *"What if he doesn't take this away?"*

The fear in this question culminated from lies. The biggest lie was that my God wasn't bigger than my sufferings.

God spoke to me through Paul: "may you be strengthened with all power, according to his glorious might, for all endurance and patience with joy, giving thanks to the Father who has qualified you to share in the inheritance of the saints in light" (Colossians 1:11,12).

I felt as if Paul's prayer for the Colossians was being prayed over me, and the more I read, the more I was convicted.

I saw that my half-faith was placing hope in momentary comfort and happiness. Paul reminded me that full-faith banks EVERYTHING on the hope of eternal salvation through Christ. And "everything" includes my pain.

God was showing me all along that he loved me and was offering me something better than momentary comfort. He used Colossians to show me that Jesus is before all things (including my pain), and because of that, I could find joy in the midst of suffering.

I'm not sure how I would have made it here on my own, but somehow God brought me to Colossians. And just like Paul, it was as if something like scales fell from my eyes, and I regained my sight.

How to Use This Book

When I attended Briercrest Bible College, I took a class that studied all of Paul's letters. It was one of my favorite classes while I was there. I had never studied the Bible like that before, and for someone who never really enjoyed reading it in the first place, that was a big deal! I wrote this book to give others that experience of falling in love with Scripture. To do so, I have combined and applied all of the skills that I was taught in my bible classes.

My encouragement for you: I am not any different from you. I don't have a degree. I am not a Bible scholar. I am just your everyday regular girl, and I am learning as I go. So, if I can do it, you can too! In fact, it is my prayer that God teaches you some of your own tricks to studying the Bible along the way! Are you ready to dive into Scripture with me? Awesome! Let's start with a few things you need to know about this book:

1. **It has two parts.** This is because the letter of Colossians is cleanly broken up into two parts: chapters 1 & 2 are all about Christian doctrine (Paul's teaching on what Christians believe) and chapters 3 & 4 cover Christian duties (how what they believe affects how they live).

2. **Each chapter covers a part of Colossians broken up by topic.** While there are only 4 chapters in Colossians, this book has quite a few more than that! You can read this book a chapter at a time if you would like, but it is designed so that you can work at your own pace.

3. **Each chapter begins with a key verse.** For instance, chapter one highlights a part of Colossians 1:10. If you would like to memorize these key verses, I have included memory cards in the *Index* of the book that you can cut out and place wherever you want.

4. **There is a story for every chapter.** Stories brought Scripture to life for me. I have written small scenes of Paul's life (mostly inspired by Scripture itself) that relate to what he is talking about in Colossians.

5. **Each passage we cover is directly in the text for your reference.** Please feel free to use this space to mark up, highlight, and jot notes. In fact, on the next page, I have given you an example of how I dive deeper into what Paul is saying. (There is also a card you can cut out in the Index *titled* "Questions for Studying the Bible." It may be helpful to refer to this.)

   Here are some things to look for as you read:
   * Pronouns
   * Verbs
   * Repeated words
   * lists
   * cause & effect
   * words that need further clarification

   Go ahead and try it with the second half of the passage (see if you catch anything I missed):

v. 1-2

GREETINGS

Paul, an apostle of Christ Jesus by the will of God, and Timothy our brother.
To the saints and faithful brothers in Christ at Colossae:
Grace to you and peace from God our Father.

use this space for notes

key:

◯ = pronouns (he, she, they)

▭ = verbs (action words)

◯ = repeated words

▭ = lists

▭▭ = cause & effect

▭ = needs definition

THANKSGIVING AND PRAYER

3 We always thank God, the Father of our Lord Jesus Christ, when we pray for you, 4 since we heard of your faith in Christ Jesus and of the love that you have for all the saints, 5 because of the hope laid up for you in heaven. Of this you have heard before in the word of the truth, the gospel, 6 which has come to you, as indeed in the whole world it is bearing fruit and increasing—as it also does among you, since the day you heard it and understood the grace of God in truth, 7 just as you learned it from Epaphras our beloved fellow servant. He is a faithful minister of Christ on your behalf 8 and has made known to us your love in the Spirit.

9 And so, from the day we heard, we have not ceased to pray for you, asking that you may be filled with the knowledge of his will in all spiritual wisdom and understanding, 10 so as to walk in a manner worthy of the Lord, fully pleasing to him: bearing fruit in every good work and increasing in the knowledge of God; 11 being strengthened with all power, according to his glorious might, for all endurance and patience with joy; 12 giving thanks to the Father, who has qualified you to share in the inheritance of the saints in light. 13 He has delivered us from the domain of darkness and transferred us to the kingdom of his beloved Son, 14 in whom we have redemption, the forgiveness of sins.

6. **There is a space for reflection in every chapter.** After you finish reading through the passage and marking it up, I have included a study tool that you can fill out to gather your thoughts.

7. **The discussion allows us to get into the application of what we read**. Now that we've read a few different things and have filled out the study tool, how does it all fit together? The discussion is the time where we walk through the passage together and talk about how it impacts our lives.

8. **Every chapter ends with discussion questions.** These can be just for your personal use, or if you are studying in a group, you can go over them together.

9. **There is a recap and a key verse at the end of Part One and Part Two.** I would suggest using this time to look back over everything you have studied so far. It would also be beneficial to reread Colossians 1-2 when you finish Part One, and reread the entire letter when you finish Part Two. (The key verse for each part also has its own memory card in the *Index*.)

10. **The Index has some helpful & FUN resources.** There are memory verse cards and other references that you can cut out. Some of the references include a "Timeline of Paul's Life" and a map of "What Paul's World Looked Like." There is also a little activity to make your own bookmarks.

Wondering how to begin?

I would suggest reading through the entire letter of Colossians and jotting down a few notes. Then ask God to give you wisdom and discernment when it comes to understanding his word. If you don't have a personal relationship with God yet, but you are interested in learning more, we talk about what Christians believe starting in chapter 1. If you believe what is said and would like to accept Jesus as your God and Savior, seek out another believer who can walk you through this prayer and what it means for your life:

> *"Heavenly Father, I have sinned against you. I want forgiveness for all my sins.*
> *I believe that Jesus died on the cross for me and rose again. Father, I give you my life to do*
> *with as you wish. I want Jesus Christ to come into my life and into my heart.*
> *This I ask in Jesus' name. Amen."*

The amazing part is that this prayer applies to Christians whether you are an "old" Christian or a "young" one. Obviously, if you are already a Christian and have asked Jesus to come into your life, he is already there, but we all need help at times reminding our hearts to draw closer to him. I think this prayer is a good place for all of us to begin. And you know what? This prayer leads right into our first chapter.

PART ONE

COLOSSIANS CHAPTERS 1 & 2
(DOCTRINE)

Walk in a manner worthy of the Lord

(Colossians 1:10)

Rome, sometime in A.D. 60-62

There was a man named Epaphras.

He was a normal man just like any other, hardly distinguishable. Paul thought of him at times, remembering the first time they met in Ephesus. When the guard told Paul that he had a visitor and Epaphras stepped into the room, Paul instantly recognized his smile, the creases in the corners of his eyes, his voice.

Epaphras looked upon Paul with compassion. His condition was fair, considering the situation. At least the guard treated him with respect and he was able to live in his own rented place. If one did not see the chains that bound him, they would not have thought anything of imprisonment. But Paul was imprisoned. He was kept from teaching about Jesus all over the world, which was his desire. All of that aside, and despite his sufferings, Paul had joy.

Epaphras and Paul met a few years earlier in Ephesus. He heard Paul teaching about Jesus and something within him was stirred, which led him to be saved. Evidently he was also trained and prepared by Paul to plant a church in Colossae, Epaphras' hometown.

There was some catching up that had to be done before Epaphras explained to Paul of the real purpose to his visit.

"The church in Colossae is doing well," he said. "They have faith in Jesus and have much love for one another. Just as the gospel is spreading throughout the world, it is spreading among them."

Paul sensed a "but" was coming.

"But–" Epaphras trailed off, searching for the words– "I have come to you seeking help with combatting some false teaching that is seeping into the church. I need your help pointing them back to the truth." [1]

GREETINGS

v. 1-2

Paul, an apostle of Christ Jesus by the will of God, and Timothy our brother.
To the saints and faithful brothers in Christ at Colossae:
Grace to you and peace from God our Father.

THANKSGIVING AND PRAYER

3 We always thank God, the Father of our Lord Jesus Christ, when we pray for you, **4** since we heard of your faith in Christ Jesus and of the love that you have for all the saints, **5** because of the hope laid up for you in heaven. Of this you have heard before in the word of the truth, the gospel, **6** which has come to you, as indeed in the whole world it is bearing fruit and increasing–as it also does among you, since the day you heard it and understood the grace of God in truth, **7** just as you learned it from Epaphras our beloved fellow servant. He is a faithful minister of Christ on your behalf **8** and has made known to us your love in the Spirit.

9 And so, from the day we heard, we have not ceased to pray for you, asking that you may be filled with the knowledge of his will in all spiritual wisdom and understanding, **10** so as to walk in a manner worthy of the Lord, fully pleasing to him: bearing fruit in every good work and increasing in the knowledge of God; **11** being strengthened with all power, according to his glorious might, for all endurance and patience with joy; **12** giving thanks to the Father, who has qualified you to share in the inheritance of the saints in light. **13** He has delivered us from the domain of darkness and transferred us to the kingdom of his beloved Son, **14** in whom we have redemption, the forgiveness of sins.

today is:

I am grateful for:

I am praying for:

SCRIPTURE TO REMEMBER:

observations:

application:

PRAYERFUL RESPONSE:

discussion

Paul always has a lot to say. Sometimes it's easy to imagine him pacing back and forth with his chains clanking and scraping along the floor as he dictates his thoughts to Timothy, scribbling away in the corner. When studying his letters it's easy to lose his main train of thought among all the commas and semicolons, but when you really take the time to break it down-sometimes word by word--you'll find there is so much to learn. This book is designed in a way where you can study the passages with me. Go ahead and mark it up to your heart's content. If you would like to learn a couple tricks for studying the scripture, you can find that in the section labeled "How to Use This Book." There we can walk through some basic hermeneutics of studying scripture together.

Once you've marked up the passage, let's begin just as Paul does: with thanksgiving and prayer. Take a moment to thank God for this letter and ask him to open your eyes to what he wants you to see.

> "We always thank God, the Father of our Lord Jesus Christ, when we pray for you." (1:3)

Paul expresses his gratitude for their faith in Jesus, their love for other Christians, and the hope they have (1:4,5). Paul shows us that this is not just any hope. This hope is "laid up," or "reserved" for them in heaven. 2

What exactly is this hope? Paul says that they have "heard" of it in the gospel.

Often times we lose the power of words like "gospel" because we say them so much and stop thinking about what they mean. Let's try to unpack this powerful word and let its meaning enrich our lives. We all need the reminder.

"Gospel" in Greek is *euaggelion* (from *eu*, "good"+ *aggelos*, "messenger"). It is best translated as "good news." [3]

What's the news and why is it so good?

Good News

No news is good news--as the saying goes. Why do we say this? Because we live in a world where our news is usually bad news. We tire of watching it on TV because pretty much the only thing that's news-worthy is broken and messed up. Where is the justice? Where is the peace? Where is the hope? Humanity has been asking this from the very beginning.

This "good news" that Paul speaks of is that justice, peace, and hope has come.

The gospel is:

    * good news
    * about Jesus
    * who came to save us from our sins
    * so that we can live new life

** *Please note that there is much more to the gospel than these four points. If you want to dive deeper into the gospel, Paul goes into more detail about it in Ephesians 1:3-14. If you haven't read the Bible before, "The Gospels" (the first four books of the New Testament: Matthew, Mark, Luke, and John) will familiarize you with Jesus Christ. Mark is a good place to start because it is quick and fast-paced and chronicles what Jesus did. John is good to read after Mark because it tells us about what Jesus said and who he is.* **

Paul says that the story of Jesus is spreading both in the world and among those in Colossae. The gospel is "bearing fruit and increasing" (1:6). What does this mean?

Bearing Fruit and Increasing

Paul is writing this letter to people who heard the story of Jesus and believed. However, this isn't news that permits them to continue living the way they did before. This is a whole new way of life and it offers us the chance to grow everyday. If the gospel was bearing fruit and increasing in the church at Colossae, it means that they were striving to know more and more about it and how it applied to their lives.

Paul shows us a very effective way to be a leader in this next part. Instead of jumping right out and criticizing the members of the church in Colossae, he encourages them first. This is a great formula we can all learn to follow when it comes to being a leader: **encouragement before correction**. We can also learn from Paul's way of correction too. He doesn't flat-out rebuke them; he prays for them. I don't doubt for a moment that Paul prayed every one of these words, without stopping. As godly leaders, we should be genuinely praying just like this:

"we have not ceased to pray for you, asking that you may be filled with the knowledge of his will in all spiritual wisdom and understanding, so as to walk in a manner worthy of the Lord fully pleasing to him: bearing fruit in every good work and increasing in the knowledge of God; being strengthened with all power, according to his glorious might, for all endurance and patience with joy; giving thanks to the Father, who has qualified you to share in the inheritance of the saints in light." (1:9-12)

We know that Epaphras came to Paul because the Colossian church was being invaded by false teaching. Paul tells the Colossians how he prays for them—and *this is how he corrects them.*

When we look at this prayer, it is much more encouraging than saying "You Colossians are not filled with the knowledge of God's will or bearing fruit in good works or relying on him to strengthen you to endure with patience and joy, nor are you thankful for God qualifying you to share in the inheritance of the saints in light."

How we lead says a whole lot about who put us in charge. If we want to be reflecting the character of God, we need to remember this. Because no matter what (whether you think you're a leader or not) there's always someone watching you. Do you want to be an encouraging leader? Pray these same things for yourself, friends. **And don't stop.**

Re-read these verses. Slowly. Let it sink in. Say it aloud, write it out, whatever you have to do for the words to come together in your head. For me it takes reading and re-reading, writing and re-writing, and a whole lot of Blue Letter Bible searches.

Paul prays that the Colossians will:

1. be filled with knowledge and understanding of God's will
2. bear fruit in good works
3. increase in the knowledge of God
4. be strengthened with God's power to endure this life
5. give thanks to God because of their hope in heaven

These are very big things. These are things we should be actively praying for and pursuing in our own lives.

This list raises a few questions. How do we do these things? How do we know God's will? What are considered "good works?"

The most important thing to note is that we cannot do any of these things in our own strength. However, God has given us a few tools to be able to chase after these things. He sent us his Holy Spirit and gave us his Word--the Bible. We also have the gift of community found in the Church, which God uses to encourage these things.

So when Paul prays that the Colossians would be able to live a life that is "worthy of the Lord" (1:10), he isn't saying that they can do anything in their own strength to be worthy. Because no matter what, the Colossians, Paul, you, and I are going to fall short of being worthy. On our own, we are not worthy of his love, or his grace, or his sacrifice.

But here is the beautiful part, we find our worth in our unworthiness. Even though we didn't deserve it, God still "delivered us from the domain of darkness and transferred us to the kingdom of his beloved Son, in whom we have redemption, the forgiveness of sins" (1:13,14). How is it that a God so big and just is able to pour out grace upon an unworthy batch of sinners? The sacrificial act of allowing his own Son to die in our place says a whole lot about what we mean to him. Even though we are unworthy of redemption, we have received it because Jesus is worthy. He lived a perfect life and paid the price we owe because of our sin. This is called GRACE. This is why we have hope reserved for us in heaven!

The Colossians were experiencing false-teaching that was trying to tell them otherwise. This is just the beginning of Paul encouraging them and leading them back to the truth.

Discussion Questions:

1. Let's walk through Colossians 1:9-14 together and unpack what Paul is saying:

   a) How can we know what God's will is (v. 9)?

   b) Take a look at Galatians 5:22,23. With this in mind, what does it look like to "bear fruit" and "increase" in the knowledge of God (v.10)?

   c) What is our "inheritance" according to verses 12-14?

2. How can you pray a prayer of encouragement for someone in your life that needs correction?

Worship. Go to youtube.com and listen to "My Worth is Not in What I Own" performed by Bethany Dillon Barnard. Let the words wash over you as you open your heart to worship.

CHAPTER 2 :

HE IS FIRST

Continue in the Faith

(Colossians 1:23)

Antioch in Pisidia, 48 A.D.

Brothers, if you have any word of encouragement for the people, say it."

Barnabas watched as Paul slowly rose to his feet from his crouched position on the floor. Paul's outstretched fingers trailed along the image of the crowd before him. To every onlooker, he appeared strong and confident. Only Paul knew how hard his heart was thumping in his ears, or how loud his breathing sounded, or how his knees trembled. He silently prayed for words, and God gave them to him.

"Men of Israel and you who fear God, listen," he called out, eyes darting from face to face scattered throughout the synagogue. "The God of Israel chose our fathers and made them a nation of great people during their time of suffering in Egypt and then he led them out of it. And for forty years he put up with them in the wilderness and finally led them to the land he had promised them. All of this took about 450 years. After that, he gave them judges. When the people asked for a king, he gave them Saul for forty years. And then he removed him and put David in his place and testified, 'I have found in David the son of Jesse a man after my own heart, who will do all my will.' As God promised, he gave to you a Savior through David's offspring, Jesus."

Paul went on to explain how John the Baptist proclaimed that the Kingdom of God was coming and called the Jews to repent of their sins. He explained that John the Baptist paved the way for Jesus. Paul paused and felt chills coursing across his arms as the room was intently silent. His eyes darted from the eyes of one man to another. He knew God was working within them.

"Brothers, sons of the family of Abraham," he continued, after a deep breath. "And to those of you who fear God, to us has been sent the message of this salvation. The prophecy of a messiah was fulfilled when those who lived in Jerusalem and its rulers condemned Jesus to death on a cross. Although they found him innocent of any crime worthy of death, they asked Pilate to have him executed. And so he was killed on a tree and laid in a tomb. But God raised him from the dead, and for many days he appeared to those who had come with him from Galilee, and they are now his witnesses. And we bring you the good news that what God promised to the fathers, this he has fulfilled to us by raising Jesus from the dead."

Paul paused as a murmur went through the crowd.

"Let it be known to you, brothers, that through Jesus forgiveness of sins is proclaimed to you, and by him everyone who believes is freed from everything which you could not be freed by the law of Moses."

The people stood and crowded around Paul and Barnabas, and many of them followed the pair out of the synagogue.

Paul never would have imagined that the story of Jesus and the Good News would have so dramatically changed his life like this. He had been changed for the better and his greatest desire was for everyone to experience the same thing. Throughout his missionary journeys, he was discovering that the first step for new life started with the knowledge of Jesus. He knew that once everyone had a solid understanding of Jesus and the gospel, the rest (the wisdom, spiritual growth, and character) would follow. 1

v. 15-16

He is the image of the invisible God, the firstborn of all creation. For by him all things were created, in heaven and on earth, visible and invisible, whether thrones or dominions or rulers or authorities—all things were created through him and for him.

17 And he is before all things, and in him all things hold together. **18** And he is the head of the body, the church. He is the beginning, the firstborn from the dead, that in everything he might be preeminent. **19** For in him all the fullness of God was pleased to dwell, **20** and through him to reconcile to himself all things, whether on earth or in heaven, making peace by the blood of his cross.

21 And you, who once were alienated and hostile in mind, doing evil deeds, **22** he has now reconciled in his body of flesh by his death, in order to present you holy and blameless and above reproach before him, **23** if indeed you continue in the faith, stable and steadfast, not shifting from the hope of the gospel that you heard, which has been proclaimed in all creation under heaven, and of which I, Paul, became a minister.

today is:

I am grateful for:

I am praying for:

SCRIPTURE TO REMEMBER:

observations:

application:

PRAYERFUL RESPONSE:

discussion

In the last part of Colossians that we read, Paul wrote that Jesus had "delivered" the Colossians into the eternal kingdom of God. In our passage today, Paul is reminding them how this is possible by emphasizing two very important things about Jesus: his divinity and the sufficiency of his sacrifice.

Verses 15-20 are often referred to as "The Hymn of Christ" because this passage is written in a way that is similar to a hymn or confession of faith at the time of early Christianity. 2 This hymn reminds us what is at the core of Christian beliefs and proclaims the new identity freely offered to all who believe.

Let's break down this confession of faith into a few points on the next page.

	SCRIPTURE (vv. 15-20)	DEFINITIONS
1	Jesus is the **image** of God.	**"image"** : *eikōn*, "likeness, representation, resem-blance."
2	Jesus is the **firstborn** of all creation.	**"firstborn"** : *prōtokos*, "first begotten"
3	Jesus **created** everything.	**"created"** : *ktizō*, "to form, shape, i.e. to completely change or transform"
4	Everything was created **through** and **for** Jesus.	**"through"** : *dia*, "the instrumental cause" **"for"** : *eis*, "intent, purpose"
5	Jesus is **before** all things.	**"before"** : *pro*, "prior to all created things in time"
6	Jesus **holds** everything **together**.	**"hold together"** : *synistēmi*, "to put together, unite, consist"
7	Jesus is the **head** of the Church.	**"head"** : *kephalē*, "supreme, chief, prominent"
8	Jesus is the **beginning**, the firstborn from **the dead**; Jesus is **preeminent**.	**"beginning"** : *archē*, "first in a series, the leader" **"the dead"** : *nekros*, spiritually dead **"preeminent"** : *prōteuō*, "to be first, hold the first place"
9	The **fullness** of God is in Jesus.	**"fullness"** : *plērōma*, "that which is filled; abundance"
10	God **reconciled** all things through Jesus' death on the cross.	**"reconcile"** : *apokatallassō*, "to bring back a former state of harmony"

*All definitions in this chart come from *Strong's Expanded Exhaustive Concordance of the Bible.*

Whatever false teaching was eating its way into the church in Colossae, it seems that it sought to greatly undermine who Christ is and what he did. It probably questioned Jesus' divinity and humanity, and the sufficiency of his salvation.

I can imagine Paul jumping up to his feet while Epaphras was telling him about this false teaching and saying to Timothy, "Grab your pen, this must be dealt with immediately!"

The first thing we must believe when we look at these points is that Jesus is a part of the Trinitarian God (God the Father, the Son, and the Holy Spirit), and that he is also human at the same time. This is difficult to understand, but Paul shows us that Christian faith banks everything on this fact. Paul led up to this in our last passage:

> "He has delivered us from the domain of darkness and transferred us to the kingdom of his beloved Son, in whom we have redemption, the forgiveness of sins." (1:13-14)

If we believe that we have been saved from the consequences that we deserve because of our sin—that we have been "born again" into a new spiritual life—we must also believe *everything* that is said about Jesus in verses 15-20.

So what is Paul saying in "The Hymn of Christ" passage? Let's look at a brief summary:

1. Jesus is **God** (points 1 & 9).
2. Jesus is **preeminent** (points 2, 5 & 8).
3. Jesus is the **Creator** (points 3,4 & 6).
4. Jesus is the **Reconciler** (points 8 & 10).
5. Jesus is the "**Re-creator**" (points 7 & 8).

This is where we find the gospel—or Good News—that we talked about in the first chapter. We have to believe these things about Jesus to have a correct understanding of the Christian faith. We must also believe these things about us:

1. We were created by God.
2. We chose to sin instead of obeying God.
3. Our sin separates us from God.

4. The consequence of our sin is death (eternal separation from God).
5. We need a Savior to restore our relationship with God.

When we believe that Jesus is our Savior, it's as if we are "re-created" or born again. It's like we are breathing from new lungs, seeing from fresh eyes. We have been made BRAND NEW!

The Colossians already knew this. But sometimes when we know something for long enough, we forget to let it affect us. Paul started out this letter praying continuously for the Colossians to be filled with this knowledge. The Good News should ALWAYS affect us!

Jesus is Before All Things

"He is before all things" (v. 17) has become a powerful, life-giving statement for me. In the times when I am overwhelmed by things of this earth (creation) like physical pain, discontentment with a job, financial stress, confusion, loss of direction, et cetera, this statement holds so much power. No matter what I am facing, I can say with all confidence that HE IS BEFORE IT!

Here, the word "before" is *pro* in Greek which means "in front of" or "prior"). The image I see when I think of this as I am facing some kind of suffering or doubt is Jesus standing in front of it. Our first reaction when facing trials is to blur out Jesus and focus on what's behind him. What would it look like if we did the opposite? Focus on Jesus. That is what Paul is reminding us to do in this passage.

In verses 15-20, Paul lists all the ways that Jesus is before all things. He is before physical creation:

> "He is the image of the invisible God, the firstborn of all creation. For by him all things were created..." (1:15)

And he is before *spiritual* creation:

> "And he is the head of the body, the church." (1:18)

This means that we have no reason to fear. Paul reminds us that Jesus holds *everything* in his hands: everything on earth and in heaven, visible and invisible, thrones, dominions, rulers, authorities–

everything (v. 16). Remember this: the world cannot throw ANYTHING at you that is bigger than God! I let fear get the better of me all the time, and the evil one tries to discourage me with lies. The biggest lie we can let seep in is one that makes us believe that God isn't bigger than something we are facing. But our passage shows us at least TEN ways that he is.

Paul also shows us what we have to look forward to: on the day of judgement, we will be presented before God holy, blameless, and above reproach because of Jesus' sacrifice. **But**, Paul tells them that they have to continue in the faith, standing firm in the gospel. This means all false teaching must be banished, all fear must be put in its place, and all sin must be confessed. This means that before anything else in your life, JESUS comes first.

Discussion Questions:

1. Name one thing in your life that you are allowing to come before Jesus. What can you do to not let that happen?

2. In this passage Paul turns our attention to Christ. Look at Paul's description of Jesus and compile a list of his character and position.

3. What is the relationship between:

   a) Jesus and the invisible God (v. 15)?
   b) Jesus and creation (**Define** firstborn) [v.16]?
   c) Jesus and the Church (v. 18)?

4. **Define** reconcile. Compare and contrast our condition before we were reconciled (v. 21) and after we were reconciled (v. 22). Do you live your daily life believing this change has happened to you?

Him we Proclaim

(Colossians 1:28)

Jerusalem, around 32 A.D.

The first stone felt as if it split his arm in two.

The second knocked the breath out of his lungs. By the third time a stone hit Paul, his eyesight began to dim.

Paul closed his eyes as his body writhed in agony and the image he saw in the dark of his mind brought him to tears. He watched a scene that he had tried to rid himself of for many years, a scene that often robbed him of his sleep.

There was Stephen, young and full of grace and power with a head of curly dark hair. A crowd was all around him, and they began hurling stones at his body. Now, Paul could feel each stone. As blood and tears poured down his face, Stephen gazed up into the sky.

"Behold," he said with a smile. "I see the heavens opened, and the Son of Man standing at the right hand of God."

At the time, Paul had just stood there; he was the one who made it all happen. But ever since he had met Jesus on the road to Damascus, this scene in his memory became a nightmare. Every night he cried out in anguish as he watched the crowd stone Steven.

"Lord Jesus, receive my spirit," Stephen had cried out. He fell to his knees. "Lord, do not hold this sin against them."

These were Stephen's last words.

Paul remembered how angry he had been when Stephen had said this. But now, at his own stoning, he felt the same pain and suffering of Stephen, whom *he* had sentenced to death. *Now* he understood. Just like Stephen, sharing the good news of Jesus and his sacrificial love was more important to Paul than anything, even death. When Paul pictured the blood on Stephen's face, he imagined the blood of Jesus.

Paul experienced more pain and suffering than most people combined. However, Paul did not think of it that way. He saw his sufferings as something that helped him know Christ more. Any time he was faced with opposition, it wasn't a surprise to him. Jesus himself told his followers that they would suffer because of their faith in him. One thing Paul had learned about suffering was that God gave him strength to rejoice in the midst of it. God also showed Paul that the times of suffering equipped him to encourage others. [1]

v. 24

Now I rejoice in my sufferings for your sake, and in my flesh I am filling up what is lacking in Christ's afflictions for the sake of his body, that is, the church,

25 of which I became a minister according to the stewardship from God that was given to me for you, to make the word of God fully known, 26 the mystery hidden for ages and generations but now revealed to his saints. 27 To them God chose to make known how great among the Gentiles are the riches of the glory of this mystery, which is Christ in you, the hope of glory. 28 Him we proclaim, warning everyone and teaching everyone with all wisdom, that we may present everyone mature in Christ. 29 For this I toil, struggling with all his energy that he powerfully works within me.

For I want you to know how great a struggle I have for you and for those at Laodicea and for all who have not seen me face to face, 2 that their hearts may be encouraged, being knit together in love, to reach all the riches of full assurance of understanding and the knowledge of God's mystery, which is Christ, 3 in whom are hidden all the treasures of wisdom and knowledge. 4 I say this in order that no one may delude you with plausible arguments. 5 For though I am absent in body, yet I am with you in spirit, rejoicing to see your good order and the firmness of your faith in Christ.

today is:

I am grateful for:

I am praying for:

SCRIPTURE TO REMEMBER:

observations:

application:

PRAYERFUL RESPONSE:

discussion

Most of us attribute the benefits of Christianity to how the faith changes our lives for the better. However, this is problematic when our lives *don't* get better. In a world where we are constantly hurt, disrespected, discouraged, lost, afraid, and face all the heartache imaginable, we often are disillusioned by this. If you became a Christian for a better way of living, you may have experienced a rude awakening. The fact is, the devoted Christian life is NOT easy. So, when Paul reminds the Colossians of "the hope of the gospel" (1:23), he isn't talking about something that is going to take away all the pain here on earth. Paul shows them that he is suffering, and being a follower of Jesus doesn't make our life better on earth. BUT, being a follower of Jesus makes all the difference for what's to come AFTER this life.

After this life we will be presented before God as "holy, blameless, and above reproach." We talked about this last time. Paul exhorted the Colossians to stand firm in the faith, even when the going gets tough. Maybe you're feeling the fire right now. Maybe you're having a hard time even standing. If you are, what Paul has to say next is what you need to hear!

It's time that we have a proper understanding of suffering. In our passage, Paul is turning the tables; he offers his circumstances as an example of how to face suffering.

"Now," he says. "This is how we should respond to trials."

Remember those false teachers? Yeah, the Colossians did too. In fact, it wouldn't surprise me if the false teachers not only sought to undermine Jesus, but they even tried to undermine Paul. Because, if they were trying to preach a "gospel" of prosperity and works, Paul was the antithesis.

They probably said something like this: "Why would you want to listen to this Paul guy? He's in prison! You can trust us, not a jailbird!"

But Paul puts them in their place:

"Now I rejoice in my sufferings for your sake, and in my flesh I am filling up what is lacking in Christ's afflictions for the sake of his body, that is, the church."
(1:24)

This is a bold statement. And it's also a little confusing. It almost sounds like Paul is saying Jesus' "afflictions" are lacking something. But how can this be when he just spent so much time explaining how Jesus' afflictions and sacrifice were completely enough to satisfy our debt and atone for our sins?

It was helpful for me to look at a different translation of this verse: "I am glad when I suffer for you in my body, for I am participating in the sufferings of Christ that continue for his body, the church," (1:24, NLT).

Sounds totally different, right? But, they're saying the same thing. This time, ESV is more difficult to understand.

"What is lacking in Christ's afflictions" is saying that Christ's afflictions are not yet complete. Paul says his own afflictions are helping complete Jesus'. Doesn't Jesus' suffering and sacrifice need to be complete for us to be redeemed?

There is a theological concept called the "already-not yet." [2] This paradigm was developed to help explain the kingdom of God and how Christians experience it. It explains how our works here on earth are a part of the advancement of the kingdom of God, but the kingdom of God in its entirety has not been totally realized. Christians are "already" apart of the kingdom of God, but they have "not yet" experienced it in its total glory.

The same goes for our reconciliation. We are "already" reconciled, but we are "not yet" seeing it in its entirety.

Before Jesus ascended into heaven after his resurrection, he commissioned his disciples to go out tell everyone what happened (Mark 16:14-20). If he didn't do this, the story of the gospel would have ended right there. The followers of Jesus are taking part in his story, because it is not yet over.

Since we are still waiting for the total revealing of God's kingdom, there is still sin in this world. There is still brokenness, ugliness, and corruption. And unfortunately, there is still suffering.

Paul tells the Colossians that suffering does not go about without purpose. He **rejoices** in his own suffering because it is helping advance the kingdom of God. What would our response to suffering look like if we had the same outlook? *How can we have this outlook?*

And Again I Say, Rejoice

"Rejoice" is *chairō*, which means "to be 'cheer'ful, i.e. calmly happy or well-off." [3]

When I was at my lowest, I hated seeing this word. I hated it because I was afraid to give my pain to God. I feared that the moment I handed it over, God wouldn't take it away and he would call me to find joy in the middle of my suffering. But instead of trusting him and remembering that he is good, I was acting as if he didn't know what was best.

Paul showed me that I COULD rejoice in the midst of suffering because it was helping advance the kingdom of God. Before I came to this realization, I was struggling with an autoimmune disease that was causing a lot of physical pain. I didn't want to have it anymore. I prayed so hard for healing that never came. At this point, I was faced with two options: giving up or standing firm.

I realized I didn't want to give up.

If anyone knows how to stand firm in the faith, it's Paul. The trials we face rock us. Paul shows us we can stand firm in the middle of the earthquake by rejoicing.

It's like walking a tightrope. If you focus on what's threatening you below, you're going to lose your balance and fall.

In the middle of suffering it's really hard to see anything to be joyful about. But Paul has already given us a pretty good list:

    1. Jesus is before all things (1:17).
    2. God has saved us from our sins (1:22).
    3. We have hope (1:27).

The first thing I had to do to be able to rejoice in my suffering was take my eyes off of it. I was focusing all my attention on the scary mess below me that it was throwing off my balance and I was starting to fall. I had to take a deep breath, fix my footing, and LOOK UP. On the other side of the rope stood Jesus, and a whole crowd cheering me on.

Continuing on with our reading, we get to add one more thing to that list:

    4. We are not alone (2:2).

Iron Sharpens Iron

"I became a minister according to the stewardship from God that was given to me for you, to make the word of God fully known." (1:25)

You are a minister.

It doesn't matter if you want to be one or not. It doesn't matter if you think you don't have the right qualifications or the time. As a follower of Christ, you are a minister!

Paul became a minister "according to the stewardship from God." The "stewardship" (*oikonomia*, meaning "dispensation, commission") that God gave to Paul is also known as "The Great Commission." [4] Although Paul wasn't one of the disciples present in Matthew 28, Paul received the same mission in Acts 13. And when you become a Christian, the same mission becomes yours: "to make the word of God fully known."

Once, the word of God was a mystery (v.26), but God revealed it not only to his people (the Jews) but to everyone. Paul says that God chose to make it known among the Gentiles too! What is the mystery? Verse

27 tells us:

> *"To them God chose to make known how great among the Gentiles are the riches of the glory of this mystery, which is Christ in you, the hope of glory."*

The glorious "mystery" is that Jesus is in us, and this is the "hope of glory." This was a radical thought for the first century Christians. Jesus did not only come to redeem the relationship between God and the Jews, but between God and ALL people. It isn't so hard to wrap our minds around today because we hear it all the time. However, what would it have looked like if God did send the Messiah to save only the Jews, as they thought was going to happen? For most of us, it's a scary thought.

Salvation freely given to anyone who believes? Now that is why we share the gospel! That is why we are ministers. And that is why Paul endured suffering with joy.

And here's where we get back to the 4th reason why we can have joy in the middle of suffering: we are not alone, because we are all apart of the same body.

When you are suffering, it is not without purpose. In fact, our suffering can majorly impact those around us. Maybe you won't know that purpose in this life, but we can be encouraged knowing that God is doing something with it.

It is encouraging to know you're not the only one struggling with a certain trial. That's why we share our testimonies with others. What would it look like if we all had the same mentality as Paul:

> *"I want you to know how great a struggle I have for you [so that your] hearts may be encouraged, being knit together in love, to reach all the riches of full assurance of understanding and the knowledge of God's mystery, which is Christ, in whom are hidden all the treasures of wisdom and knowledge." (2:1-3)*

It would look like a community that is:

1. encouraging,
2. knit together in love,
3. fully assured in understanding and knowledge of Christ,
4. and growing and maturing

And that community has these things EVEN WHEN it's hurting. In fact, it has these things EVEN MORE in the midst of suffering.

When we rejoice in our sufferings like Paul, we proclaim Jesus to our world (v.28). And we "struggle" to make Jesus known because we know what's at stake.

Jesus' sacrifice made a way for EVERYONE to be saved. For this we toil. For this we stand firm.

Don't let anyone "delude you with plausible arguments" as Paul says in 2:4. The false teachers tried to convince the Colossians that suffering wasn't worth it and that they had better things to offer. We hear the same lies everyday. But Paul says our suffering IS worth everything. And NOTHING in our world can even come close to offering what Jesus can. The benefits of being a Christian *do* change our lives for the better, but that's because we know we only have a glimpse of what's to come.

Discussion Questions:

1. What is one thing in your life right now that is causing you to suffer?

2. How did Paul view his suffering (v. 24)? How can we adopt this same attitude?

3. **Define** mystery (v.26, 27). What is the mystery God chose to make known? And who did he make it known to?

4. What "treasures" are hidden in Christ (2:3)? Where do we go to obtain these treasures?

Worship. Go on to youtube.com and listen to "Even If" by MercyMe. Open your heart to the words and let the hope of glory restore your soul.

God made Alive

(Colossians 2:13)

Jerusalem, 34 A.D.

We cannot have these people blaspheming the name of the Lord anymore," Paul exclaimed. His body was shaking with rage. He looked the high priest in the eye. "Send me to the synagogues in Damascus with letters. If I find any of these blasphemers there, I will bring them back to Jerusalem, bound."

The high priest sent him on his way to Damascus with the letters in hand.

As the city slowly came into view in the horizon, Paul felt excited. He began to scheme about how he would find the ones who spoke of Jesus Christ.

Suddenly, he was surrounded by a light so bright, he couldn't pry his eyes open. He fell to the ground in terror at the booming sound of a voice.

"Saul, Saul, why are you persecuting me?"

The voice came from no one in his party. It was as if it came from the sky itself, like a bout of crashing thunder.

Paul trembled. "Who are you, Lord?"

"I am Jesus, whom you are persecuting," the voice replied. Paul still could not open his eyes in the brightness that surrounded him. "Rise and enter the city, and you will be told what you are to do."

The men around Paul helped him to his feet. He asked them where the owner of the voice had gone, for he opened his eyes and could not see. The men were astounded.

"There was no one," one man said through a chattering jaw. "There was no one, but only a voice from heaven."

Little did Paul know that as he entered the city, God was speaking to a disciple named Ananias about him. Ananias knew of Paul and his hatred for the Church.

God told Ananias, "Go to him, for he is my instrument of choice to bring my name to the Gentiles and kings and the children of Israel."

Despite his doubt and fear, Ananias listened to God's command. He would have never imagined how a man once set on destroying the Church would be changed to build it up like it had never been before.

As for Paul, stumbling along and only able to see the darkness of his mind, he had no idea what God had in store for him. For all he knew, he deserved to die. He couldn't understand how he could have been so wrong. He had fought so hard to live a holy life, but as it turned out, he was looking at it all wrong.

This was the first time he acknowledged Jesus to be who he said he was. Jesus *was* the Lord. Now he had to learn what this meant for his life and how he should live. [1]

v. 6-7

Therefore, as you received Christ Jesus the Lord, so walk in him, rooted and built up in him and established in the faith, just as you were taught, abounding in thanksgiving.

8 See to it that no one takes you captive by philosophy and empty deceit, according to human tradition, according to the elemental spirits of the world, and not according to Christ. **9** For in him the whole fullness of deity dwells bodily, **10** and you have been filled in him, who is the head of all rule and authority. **11** In him also you were circumcised with a circumcision made without hands, by putting off the body of the flesh, by the circumcision of Christ, **12** having been buried with him in baptism, in which you were also raised with him through faith in the powerful working of God, who raised him from the dead. **13** And you, who were dead in your trespasses and the uncircumcision of your flesh, God made alive together with him, having forgiven us all our trespasses, **14** by canceling the record of debt that stood against us with its legal demands. This he set aside, nailing it to the cross.

today is:

I am grateful for:

I am praying for:

SCRIPTURE TO REMEMBER:

observations:

application:

PRAYERFUL RESPONSE:

discussion

Almost 20 years ago, a girl sat in her bed and prayed a little prayer she heard at Sunday School. She prayed for forgiveness for all the naughty things she had done and asked Jesus to come into her heart. A sudden joy came over that little girl the moment she opened her eyes that she sprang up and flew down the hall. She crashed through the door to her parents' room and threw herself up on their bed, swinging on the canopy's top post like a little monkey.

"I asked Jesus into my heart!" she exclaimed, probably loud enough for the next door neighbors to hear. "Mommy! Daddy! I asked Jesus in my heart!"

This is a beautiful story of redemption. Even if it took place at 3 o'clock in the morning.

This is how I "received" Jesus. And it is a very different story from how Paul received Jesus.

When I received Christ as my Lord and Savior, I was about two years old. I don't remember much of it, and maybe what I do is just from stories that I've heard. But I *do* know Jesus was alive in my heart, fixing the things that were broken and saving me from my own selfishness. And I wasn't afraid to tell anyone; the grocery clerk, the neighbors, it didn't matter. Jesus was in my heart, and he put a fire there.

As time goes by, it's really easy to forget to stoke the fire.

It's really easy to let our hearts become numb to the truth of the Good News.

It's really easy to let all the other noise in our world be louder than Jesus's voice.

If there was anyone who never got over the gospel, it was Paul. He didn't let the fire die, or tune out the Good News, and he didn't let the sound of the world drown out Jesus.

In this part of his letter, Paul is urging the Colossians to follow suit. He is reminding them of their redemption story, reminding them of the beauty of their salvation.

Unfortunately, it seems that the Colossians were facing false teaching regarding their salvation. So far we have seen that the false teachers were calling three things into question:

1. Jesus' authority (1:15-23)
2. Paul's authority (1:24-2:5)
3. The Colossians' salvation (*you are here)

Paul is going back to Jesus' authority to prove the Colossians are completely saved:

"And you, who once were alienated and hostile in mind, doing evil deeds, he has now reconciled in his body of flesh by his death, in order to present you holy and blameless and above reproach before him, if indeed you continue in the faith, stable and steadfast, not shifting from the hope of the gospel that you heard." (1:21-23)

If we believe that Jesus had the authority to reconcile us, we must also believe that our salvation is COMPLETE. We must believe Jesus' last words on the cross: "it is **finished**." Once we believe this, we must "continue in the faith."

What does it mean to continue in the faith? How do we do so? Paul is showing us in our passage today.

How Firm a Foundation

It's really easy to skim over verses 6 and 7. In just two verses, Paul gives an excellent explanation of what continuing in the faith looks like.

> *"Therefore, as you received Christ Jesus the Lord, so walk in him, rooted and built up in him and established in the faith, just as you were taught, abounding in thanksgiving." (2:6,7)*

Rooted, built up, established. Paul is saying the same thing, just in three different ways. Stay strong in the faith. Don't let the world distract you. Again we ask, how do we do this?

Let's break it down [*words in brackets are from NASB text]:

1. "you [have] received" – *paralambanō*, "to accept or acknowledge one to be such as he professes to be" [2]

2. "so walk" – *peripateō*, "to tread all around; figuratively: to live, deport oneself, follow as a companion, be occupied with" [3]

3. "[having been firmly] rooted" – *rhizoō*, "to cause to strike root, to strengthen with roots, to render firm, to fix, establish, cause a person or thing to be thoroughly grounded" [4]

4. "[now being] built up" – *epoikodomeō*, "to finish the structure of which the foundation has already been laid" [5]

5. "established" – *bebaioō*, "to make firm, establish, confirm, make sure" [6]

When we accept that Jesus is who he says he is, we must follow his every footstep (just like Jewish students would follow their Rabbis in the 1st century: close enough to have him kick up his dust on you) and build up our faith on a firm foundation. This firm foundation can be found back in Colossians 1:15-23, but if you already forgot, Paul tells us again in the rest of our passage today.

"For in him the whole fullness of deity dwells bodily, and you have been filled in him, who is the head of all rule and authority." (2:9,10)

God saved you from a path of destruction and put you on the path to life. Here, Paul is reminding the Colossians that GOD is in them. God was pleased to be in Jesus because he was perfect. We are not perfect. The only way to reunite us to God was for Christ to pay the debt we owed. Not only was our relationship with God restored, but it was also transformed.

Jesus transformed our relationship with God by filling us. "Filled" is *plēroō* which means, "to make full, complete." 7 If you're struggling with feeling incomplete, like something is missing--whether you know Jesus or not--he will complete you.

I believed I was incomplete without Jesus when I was two. And it was really easy to believe at such a young age. As a grew up, I know God never left my side, but I started to feel like he was distant. It turns out that he wasn't the one doing the distancing--it was me. I got caught up in suffering. I got caught up in myself and my feelings. I had to be reminded of the most fundamental part about the story of Jesus to get closer to him.

Why did I accept Jesus as my Lord and Savior in the first place? Because he LOVES me. For someone who's biggest desire was to be known and be loved, this was all I needed to be complete. However, by the time I was thirteen, I was believing lies that questioned God's love for me.

One night, I was "drowning" my sorrows in the shower. The tears probably washed my face more than the water from the shower. I was lonely, lost, and broken. Out of desperation, I cried out to God, "Are you real, God? All I want is to be loved!"

When I stepped out of the shower and dried off, I looked to the bathroom mirror that was all fogged up with steam. And right in front of my eyes were three words scribbled in the condensation, dripping: "I love you."

Jesus met me in that moment--when I was at my worst. And my life has been more loss, more struggle, more pain ever since. However, it has been COMPLETE because Christ is in me. And it has been GOOD.

A New Covenant

In our passage, Paul talks about circumcision next. In Genesis, you can find the story of Abram (a.k.a Abraham) starting in chapter 12. God promised Abraham that his offspring would be as numerous as the stars (Gen. 15:5). Abraham believed him, and he waited.

During the time of waiting God established a "covenant of circumcision" with Abraham (Gen. 17:1-14). All of Abraham's offspring were to be circumcised as a part of the covenant as well. If anyone was not circumcised, it was a sign that they were not a part of God's people.

Abraham waited for a child for almost 30 YEARS. Eventually, his wife Sarah was passed the age of being able to conceive, and they still had no children. Abraham continued to believe it would happen, even after Sarah gave up. And miraculously, they had a son and named him Isaac. Can you imagine how you would feel if God suddenly told you to offer your only child as a sacrifice a couple years later? This is exactly what happened, but Abraham continued to believe even as he tied up his son and laid him across an altar. Just as he was about to slaughter Isaac, an angel appeared and stopped him. God provided a ram to be sacrificed instead of Isaac.

This story is a beautiful parallel to Jesus' sacrifice on the cross. God offered Jesus as a sacrifice instead of us. And Jesus was his only Son.

At the time Paul wrote this letter to the Colossians, there was a lot of confusion among the early Christians in regards to circumcision. Did they still need to keep this covenant with God? Paul shows us that through Jesus' death on the cross, there is no longer a need for a physical sign because God made a new covenant with the spilling of Jesus' blood (Luke 22:20).

> "In him also you were circumcised with a circumcision made without hands, by putting off the body of the flesh, by the circumcision of Christ." (2:11)

Paul talks next about baptism. Baptism is, in some sense, a sign of the new covenant God made with the Church. However, baptism and circumcision cannot be seen as exactly parallel to each other. Circumcision was a "birthright." It was performed on infants whether they wanted it or not. Also, it said nothing of a person's spiritual life.

Baptism, on the other hand, should be in close connection to a person's spiritual life. In fact, as we see in this verse, baptism follows the "circumcision of Christ" which is "putting off the body of the flesh." Baptism is a sign that the Holy Spirit has transformed our hearts. It is a sign that God made you alive.

As the humble people we are, we always try to save ourselves. We try to read the Bible more, pray more, evangelize more. We try to rack up those brownie points with God so that we will qualify. But we can't.

The only reason we are able to proclaim that we have been made alive —holy, blameless, and above reproach—is because Jesus took our place on that cross.

Some of us get caught up in shameful thinking. We think too much about who we were before we were saved. We hold on to our "debts." But God SET THEM ASIDE. He nailed them to the cross! Don't get wrapped up in shame. It's like trying to strap chains back on after you were freed from them. If you struggle with shame, let verses 13 & 14 fill your heart.

> "And you, who were dead in your trespasses and the uncircumcision of your flesh, God made alive together with him, having forgiven us all our trespasses, by canceling the record of debt that stood against us with its legal demands. This he set aside, nailing it to the cross." (2:13,14)

Let those chains fall. Follow hard after Jesus, walking in his footsteps.

The only sturdy foundation that we can build our faith on is Christ. Once you have that, there's no false teaching that can shake you enough to destroy your foundation. You may get struck down. But you won't be destroyed.

Discussion Questions

1. How can we know if something is true?

2. Define "filled" (v.10). What does it mean to be filled with the one who is the "head of all rule and authority?"

3. Compare and contrast the circumcision of the Old Testament with the circumcision Paul talks about in v. 11-12. What is the meaning of this metaphor?

4. What was the "record of debt" that stood against you, and what were its "legal demands" (v.14)?

Substance belongs to Christ

(Colossians 2:17)

Tarsus, c. 14 A.D.

Paul knew he was a godly boy. Even more so, he hoped to be a godly man soon. He knew he was faithful to the law and following all its rules and regulations. He knew that he was obedient to his parents and that he was going to live a long life because of it.

Even though he knew these things, he didn't quite know *why* he did them. He watched as his mother and all the women in the town prepared for the Sabbath. They baked and cleaned and prepared everything in advance. Paul's mother never complained, though he knew she grew tired under all the demands. He was tired just watching her.

"Father," he said, turning to face his father. "Why must we work so hard before the day of rest?"

"It is the way things are, my son," he replied. "It is our tradition. We must work hard to enjoy our rest tomorrow."

His father must have seen the confusion in his eyes because he paused in his work and set it down.

"We observe the law because our obedience allows us to participate in the holiness of God," he said.

From that moment on, Paul wanted nothing more than to be in the holiness of God and earn his favor. Little did Paul know that there was nothing he could do to earn God's favor—no matter how hard he tried.

LET NO ONE
DISQUALIFY
YOU

v. 15-16

He disarmed the rulers and authorities and put them to open shame, by triumphing over them in him. Therefore let no one pass judgment on you in questions of food and drink, or with regard to a festival or a new moon or a Sabbath.

17 These are a shadow of the things to come, but the substance belongs to Christ. 18 Let no one disqualify you, insisting on asceticism and worship of angels, going on in detail about visions, puffed up without reason by his sensuous mind, 19 and not holding fast to the Head, from whom the whole body, nourished and knit together through its joints and ligaments, grows with a growth that is from God.

20 If with Christ you died to the elemental spirits of the world, why, as if you were still alive in the world, do you submit to regulations– 21 "Do not handle, Do not taste, Do not touch" 22 (referring to things that all perish as they are used)–according to human precepts and teachings? 23 These have indeed an appearance of wisdom in promoting self-made religion and asceticism and severity to the body, but they are of no value in stopping the indulgence of the flesh.

today is:

I am grateful for:

I am praying for:

SCRIPTURE TO REMEMBER:

observations:

application:

PRAYERFUL RESPONSE:

discussion

Most of us grew up thinking that if we worked hard enough, we would be rewarded. If we studied hard for a test, we would get a better grade. If we did our chores, maybe we got an allowance. It's easy to have the same mindset when it comes to being a Christian.

The early Christians also struggled with this mindset. It was especially confusing for those who were Jews before they became Christians because this new religion was fundamentally different. In fact, it wasn't like any other religion they had seen before.

In a world where gods were accessible by altars and sacrifices, religions were celebrated with festivals, and society was a melting pot of cultures and beliefs, it's no wonder there was some confusion.

One of the biggest questions these new Christians in Colossae had was: How do we live holy lives? The first thing Paul cleared up was that Jesus and his cross trumped the "rulers and authorities" and no one can judge them when it came to religious matters. And as we discussed in earlier chapters, it was Jesus' death on the cross that made them holy, not anything they could do on their own strength. This was where the false teachers were wrong: they tried to preach a gospel of works and prosperity instead of the true gospel. And this gospel of works that they were preaching was like a competition because if you didn't work hard enough, you would lose your prize.

Let No One Disqualify You

The substance belongs to Christ.

This statement holds so much weight in our world. I imagine a scale weighing two substances: the traditions and rules of religion versus Christ himself. Which one tips the scale? Paul says Christ.

In my own life it is easy to let this world weigh on me. I take Jesus off my scale...and you can imagine what happens. This isn't just my problem; it's the human condition. In our passage today, Paul is reminding the Colossians to reweigh their scales and make sure Christ weighs most on their hearts and lives.

There is also another image here. In verses 16 & 17, Paul says that the "questions of food and drink, or with regard to a festival or new moon or a Sabbath" are a "shadow." 1 This comes from *skia* which is defined as "an image cast by an object and representing the form of that object: opposed to the thing itself." 18

"Substance" is *sōma*, "the body (as a sound whole); the thing itself which casts the shadow." 2

This verse is saying that festivals, new moons, and Sabbaths are merely shadow puppets compared to Christ. This means that the REAL prize is not gained by focusing our attention on the shadow, but on the substance itself.

The Colossians had a hard time combatting the false teaching. The text suggests that they were being taught elements of Judaism (food regulations, religious festivals, New Moon celebrations, Sabbath day) and even some mystical elements (worship of angels, visions). Paul says those who were teaching these things were false teachers because of one important thing: they were not holding fast to the "Head." What he means is that they do not have a personal relationship with Jesus Christ.

"Let no one disqualify you, insisting on asceticism and worship of angels, going on in detail about visions, puffed up without reason by his sensuous mind, and not holding fast to the Head, from whom the whole body,

nourished and knit together through its joints and ligaments, grows with a growth that is from God."
(2:18,19)

Let no one disqualify you. This is powerful.

The people who make you feel worthless–don't let them disqualify you. The one who shames you–don't let them disqualify you. Anyone who passes any judgement on you–DON'T let them disqualify you! Even if you *try* to let lies sink in and take hold of your heart, THEY CAN'T DISQUALIFY YOU!

Remember what Paul said back in 1:12: the Father has QUALIFIED you to "share in the inheritance of the saints in light." So no matter what you or anyone else says, you are qualified.

Rules Don't Change Hearts

The Colossians are turning to rules and regulations of religion instead of banking everything on faith. Paul tells them that these rules are empty. The specific rules and regulations that the false teachers were trying to enact in the church in Colossae did not build up the church and help it grow.

Paul has also been showing them throughout the whole letter how to stand up against the false teaching. He reminds them again that it takes "holding fast" to Jesus. When they do, the whole body will grow "with a growth that is from God" (v. 19).

The thing that made Christianity so radically different form any other religion at the time was that it wasn't a list of rules of how to please God and get to heaven. In fact, there is nothing we can do in our own strength that will grant us eternal life. Instead, Christianity offered freedom through a new life.

"If with Christ you died to the elemental spirits of the world, why as if you were still alive in the world, do you submit to regulations [...] according to human precepts and teachings?" (2:20-22)

This new life found with Christ has a new lifestyle. It's different from the way the rest of the world lives. And all those traditions, rules, and regulations that once applied to you in your old life have no more weight on you in this new life. Jesus came for this very reason: to set you free from the weight and burden of sin. *This* is how he made you qualified.

"These have indeed an appearance of wisdom in promoting self-made religion and asceticism and severity to the body, but they are of no value in stopping the indulgence of the flesh." (2:23).

Rules won't change our sinful nature or our hearts. The ancient Israelites saw this again and again for many, many years. This is why Jesus had to come and die on the cross in the first place.

Jesus' sacrifice brought about a whole different kind of faith than anyone had seen or experienced before. He showed his followers that it was more about the *relationship* than the rules. Jesus called out the Pharisees because their "devotion" to God was more of a show than an actual growing relationship.

Here's an example: what is the difference between doing something for someone because you *have* to, versus doing it because you *love* them? Like the thirteen-year-old that cleans his room because he knows it will make his mom happy instead of cleaning it after she asks fifty times. This action is done out of love. And *that* is what changes hearts.

You can also look at marriage: a wife and husband may have certain "chores" that they do around the house. However, when the husband does the laundry for his wife, even though it is his least favorite chore, he is showing her that he loves her and isn't just following the "rules."

God gives us the choice to be in relationship with him because he wants us to have the desire. He doesn't want a bunch of goody-two-shoes brown-nosers! And while there *are* things we should and shouldn't do, those "rules" are for our protection. However, just like cleaning our rooms before our mom has to ask, we follow the "rules" because we love God.

In our last chapter we talked about how to stand firm in the faith. The reason for standing firm in the faith is for such an occasion as the Colossians were facing. False teaching was all around them. It's not very different today. You have lots of different voices all around you. You have things trying to grab your attention and pull you in a million different directions. How do you stand firm when everything is trying to shake you down? Paul says instead of making more rules for yourself, hold fast to Jesus.

What does it mean to hold fast to Jesus?

It means the driving force for how you live is not the world, but Jesus. But wait, *how* do we do hold fast to Jesus? Don't worry, we'll talk about it in the next chapter. For now, just know the rules don't even come close to bringing out the change that a personal relationship with Christ does. They are just a shadow. The new life that Jesus offers is the **substance**.

Discussion Questions

1. Who are the "rulers and authorities" Paul talks about in v. 15, and how did Jesus "disarm" them (see Ephesians 6:12)?

2. Paul describes the rules as having no "value" in v. 23. Does this mean we no longer have rules under the gospel that restrict what we can handle, taste, or touch? How can we know if a rule is proper or not?

3. Make a list of all the things you would do for your current or future spouse to show them that you love them. Then make a list for how you could show God you love him. Are there any similarities?

4. What is the driving force for the Colossians to "walk in a manner worthy of the Lord" (1:10)?

Recap

1. Christians are called to walk in a manner worthy of the Lord (1:1-14).

2. Through Jesus' death on the cross, all people can be made holy if they believe (1:15-23).

3. Christians have joy in the midst of suffering because it is not without purpose (1:24-2:5).

4. God makes us alive with Jesus (2:6-14).

5. We are saved not through works, but through faith (2:15-23).

The first half of Colossians covers Christian doctrine and puts Jesus in his proper place. As we move on to the next half, we will discuss how these truths apply to our daily lives.

On the next page, I have highlighted a verse that speaks well to everything we have discussed in this first half of the letter. You can find cards in the back of the book with verses that highlight all the main points we discuss. They are there for you to cut out and place wherever you need the reminder.

"THEREFORE, AS YOU RECEIVED CHRIST JESUS THE LORD,
SO WALK IN HIM, ROOTED AND BUILT UP IN HIM AND
ESTABLISHED IN THE FAITH, JUST AS YOU WERE TAUGHT,
ABOUNDING IN THANKSGIVING."

COLOSSIANS 2:6-7

You can cut this page out and place it in a 8x10 frame
to display wherever you need the reminder.

PART TWO

COLOSSIANS CHAPTERS 3 & 4
(DUTIES)

Put on the New Self

(Colossians 3:10)

Jerusalem, 37 A.D.

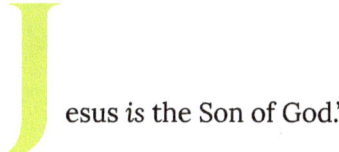esus *is* the Son of God."

A week earlier, and Paul would have been arresting whoever spoke these words. But now, his life had been changed, and they were coming from *his mouth.*

A wave of voices washed across the room in the synagogue, echoing out to the doors. Paul knew what they were saying. "Isn't this the man who made havoc in Jerusalem of those who called upon the name of the Lord? And has he not come here to bring them back to the chief priests?"

When Paul returned to Jerusalem, he was met with the same opposition by the disciples when he attempted to join them.

"You could not be a disciple with all of the evil you have done!" cried out one of the men, shaking his fist. Paul felt his heart stir within him. He did not know what to say. How would God use him if no one trusted him?

"I believe him."

Every face turned to look at the man. His name was Barnabas.

"This is a new man," Barnabas declared. "This man who was once against those who follow Jesus has now become a follower. Jesus met him on the road to Damascus. He has preached boldly in Damascus about Jesus. Do not judge this man based on his old life, or what he did before. This is a new man. He is not these things anymore."

It was in these words that Paul learned what it meant to have new life. Barnabas would show him that following the way of Jesus started with following him to the grave. And then it meant rising from the dead into a new life: a new life that was not like anything on this earth. 1

v. 1-2

If then you have been raised with Christ, seek the things that are above, where Christ is, seated at the right hand of God. Set your minds on things that are above, not on things that are on earth.

3 For you have died, and your life is hidden with Christ in God. **4** When Christ who is your life appears, then you also will appear with him in glory.

5 Put to death therefore what is earthly in you: sexual immorality, impurity, passion, evil desire, and covetous-ness, which is idolatry. **6** On account of these the wrath of God is coming. **7** In these you too once walked, when you were living in them. **8** But now you must put them all away: anger, wrath, malice, slander, and obscene talk from your mouth. **9** Do not lie to one another, seeing that you have put off the old self with its practices **10** and have put on the new self, which is being renewed in knowledge after the image of its creator. **11** Here there is not Greek and Jew, circumcised and uncircumcised, barbarian, Scythian, slave, free; but Christ is all, and in all.

today is:

I am grateful for:

I am praying for:

SCRIPTURE TO REMEMBER:

observations:

application:

PRAYERFUL RESPONSE:

discussion

God made you alive. This is what Paul preached in our last passage. In our passage today, we are seeing a continuation of this thought. Paul told the Colossians that if they were alive in Christ, they needed to live like it!

First century Christians in Colossae lived in the "suburbs." The city was mostly made up of Gentile population, though there were many Jews living in the area. Besides these, there were many cultures seeming to melt together where this small church was, and this is where the false teaching began to seep in.

Does this sound a little familiar?

While we cannot relate to everything the biblical audience was experiencing at the time when Paul wrote this letter, there are a few similarities: we are Christians living in a non-Christian world and we face "false-teaching" every day. Multiple times a day.

Just turn on your TV. Look at Facebook. Billboards, magazines, movies...you name it. We are surrounded by millions of voices that are all trying to drown out the truth and turn up the volume to our own selfish desires. We all have our "idols" and our comforts that we like to hold on to. But, just as Paul urged the Colossians, we must turn away from these.

Comfort is the biggest threat to Christians in modern day America. We like being comfortable. Unfortunately, when we are comfortable, we tend to rely on God less. We fill our days with things other than him, and a week may go by before you realize you haven't even thought about him. Comfort leads to complacent Christians, and this describes the way many Christians live in America today.

None of us like being uncomfortable or suffering, but I find that those are times when our relationships with God grow the most. I wouldn't change any hard situation that I have gone through because I know without a doubt they brought me closer to God.

So hear my encouragement for you: if you are suffering, seek Christ; If you are comfortable, seek Christ. It isn't an easy task in either situation, but it's probably even harder when everything is going good. Remember that.

> "If then you have been raised with Christ, seek the things that are above, where Christ is, seated at the right hand of God." (3:1)

Raised with Christ

When you were "raised with Christ"—when you declared Jesus Christ as your Lord and Savior—a few big things happened:

1. Your sins were forgiven.
2. You were adopted into God's family.
3. You received a new nature with new priorities.
4. You were given a new homeland.

All of these are the foundation of your identity and what makes you who you are. When you were raised with Christ, a magnificent conversion happened, causing a radical change to your foundational identity! That's why every redemption story is beautiful and powerful and why it's not about you! Now this is something that our world needs to hear, even in the 21st century!

All the things that matter to you, all the things that make you "who you are," they are no longer relevant. Because you've left all of those things behind you. And not only behind you, but *totally forgotten. It's gotta be the best fresh start you could ever ask for!*

This is what Paul means when he says your life is hidden with Christ. Your life becomes his life. **Christ is your life.** Wherever he is, you are, even in glory.

Let's just take a moment to unpack that word.

Glory:
1. high renown or honor won by notable achievements
2. magnificence or great beauty
3. Distinction

We will be glorified in Christ when we are revealed with him.

No matter what you are going through right now, whether it be sin, heartache, depression, shattered dreams, or something else that is causing you to feel like God is being silent, find your hope and courage in this: "he who began a good work in you will bring it to completion at the day of Jesus Christ" (Philippians 1:6). This means that aching feeling you have for something more will finally be filled when you go to your true home--heaven.

He gave you a whole new identity. He turned a sinful human deserving of death into a new creation, raised with Christ, who will one day appear with him in glory. Set your mind on this. Set your mind on things above.

What does this mean for us in the meantime?

If you're like me, setting my mind on something usually means it's going to happen and there's no changing my mind. So, set your mind on this truth. Even if it seems like God is silent, I promise you, he's not. Figure out how to listen to him better, ask other Christians to help you discern what God is telling you, and don't forget that **our hope is not found in this world.** Our hope is in Christ and the glory to come. This is what Paul meant when he wrote "For me to live is Christ, to die is gain," (Philippians 1:21). Our lives here on earth are going to be hard, but we are called to live them with joy because of what Christ has done. We have nothing to lose here, and EVERYTHING to gain in heaven! **This** is setting our minds on things above.

If we are setting our minds on things that are above, this means we cannot live the way we used to. Through Christ's loving sacrifice, we are no longer bound to our sins. It's ridiculous for someone to try to strap their chains back on after they've been set free, but we do it all the time! Starting at verse 5, Paul reminds the Colossians that they must obey God's commands.

Perhaps there was some false teaching that was going around in the small Colossian church that went something like this,"If God is a merciful God and I believe in him, then it's okay if I sin every once in a while because he has already forgiven me."

Paul's response is, "You're missing the point!"

He tells them to be prepared because "the wrath of God is coming" against disobedience. The wrath. That's a very powerful, emotional word.

We can also see Paul's response to this in Romans 6:1, 2: "What shall we say then? Are we to continue in sin that grace may abound? By no means! How can we who died to sin still live in it?"

Paul emphasizes that we miss the whole point of conversion when we continue to sin.

When I was young, I used to struggle with lying. I'm not sure why, but it was a big part of my sinful nature. I guess it was the natural born story-teller in me (ha ha). I think it was also borne out of insecurity. Even though I convinced myself that they were just "little white lies" and no one would find out, somehow, someone ALWAYS found out. It took time for me to realize that God was calling me out of that life. He was telling me to put it away and follow hard after him. It was like kicking a bad habit, but by the time I rededicated my life to Christ when I was thirteen, I knew I didn't want to lie anymore. It wasn't easy to stop. I know the only reason I was able to was through the work of the Holy Spirit in my heart.

"But now you must put them all away: anger, wrath, malice, slander, and obscene talk from your mouth." (3:8)

The image that I have here is an alcoholic now sober going through the cupboards and drawers and tossing out every bottle of whiskey, beer, wine, and rum they can find. Or better yet, the image of a woman put in protective custody getting rid of everything that was associated with her old identity so that she can have a fresh, new start somewhere safe.

This is the point we miss when we continue to turn back to sin after we become Christians: your old identity is not there. You died with

Christ. You are 100% totally and completely **new**. Just like when the two Mary's went to Jesus' tomb and the angel appeared: "**He is not here**, for he has risen" (Matthew 28:6). You died with Christ. And in the same way, you were raised to life again. But not the same life; you were raised to a completely new life!

But there is something even more beautiful: it was not just one act and done.

Put On the New Self

> "you have put off the old self with its practices and have put on the new self which is being renewed in knowledge after the image of its creator." (3:9,10)

Did you catch that? You are *being* renewed. This is a continuous act. This is a process. You have a new self, spirit, heart, mind, tongue, name, covenant, commandment, and song! You are made new each day; it's brand new every morning! Now this is grace. We are going to fail and make mistakes. We are going to sin. But—and this is a big but—we do not see this as an excuse to continue to live in sin. Instead, we can confess our sins and get a fresh start. And we find hope in banking everything on the fact that one day we will be with Christ, and his glory.

We have the choice to become more like Christ everyday. The more you seek him and ask him to make you more like him, the less you look like the rest of the world. In Christ, our lives are no longer defined by labels like they are in the world:

> "Here there is not Greek and jew, circumcised and uncircumcised, barbarian, Scythian, slave, free, but Christ is all, and in all." (3:11)

When you become a Christian, it doesn't matter what you look like, how you dress, where you come from, or what you have done. All of these are gone. What remains is Christ. Christ is *all*.

God's heart for the Church is new life. He is abolishing all earthly distinctions and creating unity. The things that once distinguished and separated (Greek and Jew, circumcised and uncircumcised, slave and free) are no more. Therefore, no one can boast in anything that they are or have done. What should remain is a unified body where "Christ is all and in all."

In the words of the hymn written by Stuart Townend, "I will not boast in anything, no gifts, no power, no wisdom; but I will boast in Jesus Christ, his death and resurrection."

Jesus Christ is your all in all. He is your life, your hope, your glory.

Discussion Questions

1. Why is our mind-set so crucial to our service to God?

2. List some examples of proper priorities when it comes to living like Christ.

3. How do we "put away" all the things Paul lists in v.8? Is it done all in our own strength?

Worship. Go on to <u>youtube.com</u> and give a listen to "How Deep the Father's Love For Us" performed by Selah. Let the truth wash over you and open your heart to worship.

Chosen, Holy & Beloved

(Colossians 3:12)

Antioch, 47 A.D.

Even though the room was small, it was filled with the din of
the conversing prophets, teachers and disciples. Barnabas had come
all the way to Tarsus just to find Paul and bring him back here to
Antioch almost a year before. Paul could still remember that
conversation.

"I've come to bring you with me to Antioch," Barnabas said. "Some of
those who fled from the persecution went all the way to Antioch and
spoke the word. They sent word to me while I was in Jerusalem to
come and I am very pleased to say that the grace of God is there and
we have started a church. I want you to come see it."

The church in Antioch had indeed grown in number—it seemed to
grow every day. It was here in Antioch that the disciples were known
as Christians. They all knew it was a jab—"little Christ," said the scoffers
—but they accepted it anyway.

Paul and Barnabas had grown quite close over the last year and Paul
greatly appreciated their friendship.

The church in Antioch's prophets and teachers were Barnabas, Niger,
Lucius, Manaen, and Paul. The group was fasting and worshipping the
Lord when they heard the Holy Spirit say, "Set apart for me Barnabas
and Paul for the work to which I have called them."

Me? Paul wondered. *Out of all these men, why did God choose me?*

When they finished worshiping and fasting, the other men in the
group laid their hands on Paul and Barnabas, and then they sent them
off.

"Why do you think the Lord is sending me?" Paul asked Barnabas, as he
looked back at Antioch over his shoulder.

"Our Lord has been preparing you all this time to go out and share the
news of Love, now it's time to live it out." [1]

PUT ON THE
NEW SELF

v. 12-13

Put on then, as God's chosen ones, holy and beloved, compassionate hearts, kindness, humility, meekness, and patience, bearing with one another and, if one has a complaint against another forgiving each other; as the Lord has forgiven you, so you also must forgive.

14 And above all these put on love, which binds everything together in perfect harmony. **15** And let the peace of Christ rule in your hearts, to which indeed you were called in one body. And be thankful. **16** Let the word of Christ dwell in you richly, teaching and admonishing one another in all wisdom, singing psalms and hymns and spiritual songs, with thankfulness in your hearts to God. **17** And whatever you do, in word or deed, do everything in the name of the Lord Jesus, giving thanks to God the Father through him.

today is:

I am grateful for:

I am praying for:

SCRIPTURE TO REMEMBER:

observations:

application:

PRAYERFUL RESPONSE:

discussion

We've talked about conversion. We've talked about everything that changes and what we take off when we accept Jesus Christ as our Lord and Savior, and accept that he is our all in all. Our everything. Now, we have reached the point where we discuss the new self and what it looks like. We take off the old self like a garment, and in the same way, we put on the new self like a brand new article of clothing.

In our passage, Paul lists the fruit that we should see in our lives after our radical conversion. Remember that everything that is foundational to our identity is completely new in Christ—our hearts, minds, tongues, spirits, names, et cetera. If that is true, there has to be *some* kind of change in us.

Before we get to that list, I want to take a moment to really think about the first couple words of our passage, specifically "chosen ones, holy and beloved" (v. 12). I don't want to skim over this and miss the beauty in those words.

You are God's chosen one. In Greek the word is eklektos and it means "choice, select; having excellence. ₂ He has made you his EXCELLENT ONE! God chose YOU and allowed you to obtain salvation.

What does this mean for you? It means that God saw your mess and he still CHOSE YOU. It means that God saw the worst thing you have ever done and said "I still want you, I CHOOSE YOU."

It means that even though you did not deserve salvation, even though you could do nothing to warrant God's love, he threw everything aside, sent his Son to die in your place, gave you a completely new identity, and calls you HOLY and BELOVED.

Time and time again we turn away from God and get distracted by things in this world but, as Paul reminded the Colossians, you are not of this world! Every day that you get up, feed your kids, go to work, go to school—everyday whether it is hard to get out of bed or you have the energy to run a marathon—God has called you to a higher standard of living and it **should be visible**.

Christians should have these qualities:

* Compassion
* Kindness
* Humility
* Meekness
* Patience & forgiveness in disagreements
* And above all, love

The Greatest of These is Love

Many of us were taught that the most important thing about Christianity is faith. We are reminded to be faithful again and again. This is often why we go to church, do devotions, and live godly lives. However, the higher standard of living that God is calling us to should be rooted out of love.

Without love, a faithful life is NOTHING. All the things Paul lists as good Christ-like qualities are NOTHING without love.

Hear this, Christians! Because EVERYONE sees when you are being a hypocrite. People are looking to see how you respond to the sin around you. If you respond by shooting flaming arrows of judgement based on your "faith," I can promise you that does not change hearts. What *does* change hearts is one action found in everything Jesus did: **love**.

Paul knew his actions were on display. He also knew that we all make a lot of mistakes. The same hand that wrote this letter of encouragement and preaching on love was stained with blood.

But love is even above those mistakes.

The love of Christ displayed on the cross should not only call, but compel us to put on hearts that are compassionate, kind, humble, meek, patient, and thankful. All these things are borne out of LOVING hearts. Jesus abolished the weight of law by showing us a simpler way: put on love and everything else with follow.

And how do we love? It's the basic principle that Jesus lived out every day: putting everyone else before himself.

And there is something else that is beautiful here. While you are doing your work of putting on love (because it is **your choice**), God is meeting you wherever you are and giving you two very special things: the peace and the word of Christ.

"And let the peace of Christ rule in your hearts, to which indeed you were called in one body. And be thankful. Let the word of Christ dwell in you richly, teaching and admonishing one another in all wisdom, singing psalms and hymns and spiritual songs, with thankfulness in your hearts to God" (3:15,16).

In our whole passage, Paul gives a list of commandments to God's chosen ones, and all of them are active verbs (something they do), except these two things which are passive verbs (something done to them). Therefore, the peace of Christ and the indwelling of his word in our hearts is something that Christ gives us, something that we let happen. ("The word of Christ" means doctrine concerning our salvation into the kingdom of God that we received through Christ.) Of course, all of this is connected. When we let the peace and word of Christ dwell in our hearts, we will see those other commandments start to come out.

Be Thankful

It's hard to miss the aspect of thanksgiving here. Paul says it three times in verses 15-17.

I know it's really hard to be thankful when we are caught up in our own selfish desires. But when we turn our attention off of us and to the peace and Word of Christ, that's where you can find things to be grateful for.

This is part of my own story. I was very ungrateful for my situation. Instead of giving my pain to God and being thankful for the countless blessings that surrounded me, I was frustrated and unhappy. Even though I didn't want to admit it, my husband was right. He told me to thank God for my pain. This tore me up. How could I learn to be thankful for something that was causing the most heartache in my life? I had to work my way up to it. I started small; I thanked God for what I really was thankful for and prayed for the strength to thank him for the bad things too. Eventually, my pain ended up on that list. And I was thankful for it because it reminded me of my daily--HOURLY--need of Christ.

God gave me the peace of Christ: I was able to rest in him in the midst of my suffering. And God gave me the Word of Christ: I found strength and courage by turning to the Bible and letting it pour over me.

Paul showed me the characteristics I was lacking in this passage. I had to trade in what I was "wearing" for something new. I had to put on compassion, instead of selfishness, humility instead of arrogance, patience instead of frustration, and above all, I had to put on love.

The thing is, we can't do this in our own strength. We have to fix our eyes on Christ and let him do the work. Even though Paul is telling us to do these things, we are still reliant on the Holy Spirit to do the work.

The whole point of this passage and why Paul writes this is so that the Church may be unified, or one body, as we read in verse fifteen. And if everything we do is done in the name of Jesus (who is the greatest display of love ever), we will be bound together.

Don't be overwhelmed by the list Paul gives us. Remember that Jesus abolished the rules and regulations for an easier way. Rules and regulations of faith don't change hearts. Love does.

Discussion Questions

1. What does it mean to do everything in the name of Jesus (v.17)?

2. Why is it so important to be thankful?

Apply. What does it look like to do these things in v.12-14:

	FOR OTHERS (spouse, children, friends, etc.)
COMPASSION	
KINDNESS	
HUMILITY	
MEEKNESS	
PATIENCE	
BEARING WITH	
FORGIVING	

* Notice how our loving relationships on earth reflect ways God loves us. Think of a way you can grow in your relationship with God and try to implement it in your daily life.

You are serving
the Lord

(Colossians 3:24)

Rome, 60 A.D.

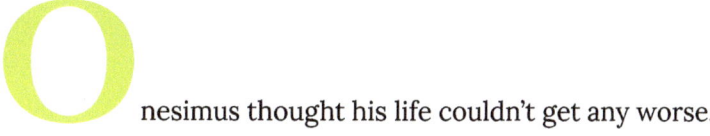nesimus thought his life couldn't get any worse.

Well, that's what he *had* thought, until this moment. Here he was in his "freedom" and he was working among prisoners just to get enough to eat that night. He couldn't believe his luck. A few months before he thought he had finally caught his break to freedom. He knew what he did wasn't right, but he told himself he had no other option.

Onesimus was once a slave. But he was a terrible slave. He hated working for someone else—all he wanted was to be the master of his own life. And so one night, he seized the opportunity. While his master Philemon slept, he snuck into his house and stole enough that would get him to Rome. His plan was to work—as a free man. As he fled, he dreamed of being just like his master one day, with his own home, land, and slaves...probably. He would work hard for that dream.

Unfortunately, he couldn't work hard enough in Rome. So here he was, gleaning after the prisoners.

"What are you doing here?"

Onesimus' head whipped around, startled. Before him stood a bent man with a sharp nose and balding head. His voice had sounded stern, but his eyes sparkled like none Onesimus had seen before. Onesimus realized this man was one of the prisoners, although he did not look like he deserved to be one.

"Working," Onesimus stuttered in reply. "To eat."

The man's eyes glimmered, "Come eat with me." He gestured with his hand and hobbled down the street.

Onesimus was surprised to find the man was permitted to rent his own place, although he was chained and watched by a guard. The guard even seemed to like him.

"Who are you?" Onesimus asked as they ate. He really was more curious about what this man had done to be a prisoner, but thought it best not to ask this.

"My name is Paul," said the man. "I was going to ask you the same thing."

"My name is Onesimus," he began, and swiftly found himself relaying his whole story to Paul, who oddly made him feel so welcome and safe. Little did Onesimus know in this moment that he would grow very close with the man before him and the life of slavery that he had run away from would only turn into a new kind of slavery. But this time, the Master he would come to serve resided in heaven. [1]

RULES FOR
CHRISTIAN
HOUSE-
HOLDS

v. 18–20

Wives, submit to your husbands, as is fitting in the Lord. Husbands, love your wives, and do not be harsh with them. Children, obey your parents in everything, for this pleases the Lord.

21 Fathers, do not provoke your children, lest they become discouraged. **22** Bondservants, obey in everything those who are your earthly masters, not by way of eye-service, as people-pleasers, but with sincerity of heart, fearing the Lord. **23** Whatever you do, work heartily, as for the Lord and not for men, **24** knowing that from the Lord you will receive the inheritance as your reward. You are serving the Lord Christ. **25** For the wrongdoer will be paid back for the wrong he has done, and there is no partiality.

4 Masters, treat your bondservants justly and fairly, knowing that you also have a Master in heaven.

today is:

I am grateful for:

I am praying for:

SCRIPTURE TO REMEMBER:

observations:

application:

PRAYERFUL RESPONSE:

discussion

When compared to our last passage, this passage may feel like an abrupt change. Some scholars argue that it must have been inserted later because it does not feel like the two thoughts flow together. However, Paul is continuing his thought about the new life, and giving some practical application to the Colossians' own lives. When Paul said to "do everything in the name of the Lord Jesus" (3:17) in our last passage, today we see that he is well aware that the people who know us the best are the ones that we have the most intimate relationships with. Especially the ones that we live with. Therefore, the purpose of this passage is still in line with the rest of his thesis, and is the practical application of the Gospel in our every moment of life.

I'm sure we can all relate to the desire of having an organized and peaceful home life. In the ancient world, it wasn't only Christians that sought harmony in their homes, Greeks also made this a priority and saw the home as the foundation for government, as was Aristotle's prevalent thought of the time. 2 Jews also had their ideals for family life from the Law. Jews and Greeks alike sought to structure their homes peacefully through a hierarchy. So this begs a question, if we are supposed to set our minds on things above and not of the world—and these roles are of the world—why is Paul giving in and abandoning his earlier declaration?

He's not. Instead, Paul is applying the Gospel to this setting, and he is not concerned with the social and legal codes, but with relationships and how they show the love of Christ. Remember that love is above all the other traits that Paul noted in the preceding passage—peace, wisdom, knowledge, forgiveness, compassion, et cetera. All of these should be in the behavior at home, not just at church.

Why would wives submit to their husbands? Because they love them. What is Paul's command for husbands? To love their wives. What causes children to obey their parents? Love. Do you see a theme? Good.

And what is to be said for slaves and masters? Do slaves love their masters or masters love their slaves? If they have been paying attention to the last two parts of the letter, then they would see that Paul is saying they should. Paul is offering an explanation of how they can live out their faith in the midst of this arrangement; they live out their faith *through love.*

Why should they live like this? Because both masters and slaves are slaves of Christ (3:24; 4:1). Paul also describes himself as such. In Romans, Paul teaches that everyone is a slave: "Do you not know that if you present yourselves to anyone as obedient slaves, you are slaves of the one whom you obey, either of sin, which leads to death, or of obedience, which leads to righteousness?" (Romans 6:16) Even though we are slaves of Jesus, ironically, this is what sets us TRULY free!

The majority of this passage is exhortations to the "bondservants" or slaves. This is because the message is applicable to all people, whether they are wives, husbands, parents, slaves, or masters.

Let's unpack the rest of our passage, starting at verse 22.

Obey Your Masters

Paul instructs the Colossians:

> *"Bondservants, obey in everything those who are your earthly masters..." (3:22a)*

"Obey" (*hypakouō*) means to follow instructions precisely. [3] This type of obedience is to be total—"in everything." However, see how Paul qualifies the statement by saying "earthly masters." Here he is saying that the masters of earth do not have ultimate authority. He does not condone servants (or wives and children as he mentions earlier) obeying ungodly commands, but only what is "fitting in the Lord" (3:18). Ultimate authority is found only in God. His commands are to be obeyed above any commands of humans.

Another thing to note in this verse is that Paul is not just speaking of outward obedience, he is also speaking of the heart—of our attitudes.

"not by the way of eye-service, as people pleasers, but with sincerity of heart, fearing the Lord." (3:22b)

Our attitude when it comes to obedience (and I think it is valid to point out our obedience to God and his command to live Godly lives) should not be done:

1. **"by the way of eye-service"** (ESV), "external service" (NASB), "when their eye is on you" (NIV), "eye-service" is *ophthalmodoulia*, "service performed [only] under the master's eyes." [4]

2. **"to win their favor"** (NIV), "those who merely please men" (NASB), "people pleasers" (ESV) is *anthrōpareskos*, "studying to please man, courting the favor of men," from *anthrōpos* "man, human" + *areskō* "to please." [5]

But, instead, out of:

1. **"sincerity"** (ESV), "wholeheartedly" (NRSV), "singleness" (KJV) is *haplotēs*, literally "singleness." [6] We see it used in the New Testament as honesty conveyed through our words and actions.

2. **and "with reverence"** (NIV), "fearing" (ESV, NASB) is *phobeō*, "to fear." Fearing the Lord means regarding him with profound respect, and a fear of offending him. [7]

Work for the Lord, Not for Men

Here is where we dive deeper into the work ethic that Christians should have:

"Whatever you do, work heartily, as for the Lord and not for men, knowing that from the Lord you will received the inheritance as your reward. You are serving the Lord Christ." (3:23-24)

I don't know how many times I've done something and didn't work as hard on it as I should have and I qualified myself by saying it was good enough. "Eh, good enough" may be a cultural attitude towards life and work, but Paul is saying our standards must be higher than that. Remember to seek things above, i.e. go above and beyond what's "acceptable." It's time to raise your "grades" to A+!

Here's a few things to note about these couple verses:

1. **"Whatever you do."** No matter the project, seek excellence. Go above and beyond—even when no one is watching.

2. **"work heartily"** (ESV, NASB), "put yourselves into it" (NRSV), "heartily" comes from *ek*, "out of" + *psychē*, "the soul." [8] The soul here refers to your "life," "breath," everything that is at the core of who you are.

3. **"for the Lord and not for men"** (ESV). This radical statement is the result of your radical conversion. You must consider every work and deed as something you are doing for God himself. Just to make sure we hear it, Paul reiterates: "You are serving the Lord Christ!"

What happens when we love others and they mistreat us? This is Paul's answer:

"the wrongdoer will be paid back for the wrong he has done, and there is no partiality." (3:25)

It's bound to happen in this sinful world. You will be mistreated. You will be mocked and scorned. But Jesus has given you two commands: Love God with all you heart, soul, and mind, and love everyone else as you would love yourself (Matt. 22:37,38). Your consolation is knowing that you have an inheritance waiting for you in heaven as your reward and those who do wrong will pay the full price.

Whether you are a wife, husband, child, father, servant, or master—if you have been given new life through the sacrifice of Jesus Christ—you are serving *him*. He knows your actions and your attitude. No matter where you are in your journey with Christ—if you know what he has called you to do for his kingdom or not—you can know this: he has commanded you to live in a way that shows he has made you a new creation. Your calling is to live out your life knowing you have a loving and just Master and Father in heaven and you will one day "receive the inheritance" of heaven. How many other slaves do you know that can say that?

Discussion Questions

1. What does it mean for a wife to submit to her husband? (Does submitting to authority mean that you are less important or less valuable?)

2. How should we respond when authoritative figures in our lives are not living "justly and fairly?"

3. What family member are you? What is your instruction for your everyday life? How can you live it out this week?

4. Are you more like a master or servant in the working world? How can you live out these truths in the workplace?

A door for the Word

(Colossians 4:3)

Seleucia, 47 A.D.

They had no idea where they were going, and it seemed to Paul that this was the way God often worked.

He, Barnabas, and Mark (Barnabas' cousin) sat near the docks in Seleucia and surveyed their surroundings. Barnabas ate a piece of fruit in quiet musing. Paul couldn't help but smile at his friend's optimism.

A wide sea before them, and countless countries to go to. Paul had no idea where to go first. But Barnabas didn't seem fazed. There he was just eating his fruit.

The three of them had been praying for God to make it clear where they were to go next, and God seemed oddly silent for just commissioning them to go out into the world. Barnabas had told them to devote themselves to their prayers, and to be vigilant. Then he told them to also be thankful while they waited. So they did for three days. Paul knew God would speak eventually, he just wondered how much longer it would take.

"Cyprus."

Paul looked at Barnabas, startled by his sudden speech.

"What?" Mark asked.

"The Lord is telling me we will go to Cyprus," answered Barnabas, wiping his hands on his cloak and rising to his feet. Paul didn't question him. He rose as well, following Barnabas to the docks. Mark was a little more hesitant, but he too followed.

"Is anyone going to the island of Cyprus?" Barnabas asked the men on the dock. This was followed by a resounding series of no's, and Paul could see Mark's doubts even clearer on his face.

Barnabas shrugged and led them off the docks. As they walked back to the place where they would stay for the night, Paul heard two men talking in the street.

"I know it's not the best season to go, but I must sail to Cyprus," said one of the men. "And I am leaving in the morning."

Paul laughed as Barnabas smiled to himself and reached out to the man.

"Do you have room for three more on your boat?"

When it came to sharing the Word with others, God always opened the door. Most of the time, however, it wasn't how they expected. Paul was learning that there were three kinds of people when it came to waiting on God: the doubter, the apathetic, and the faithful. He saw that God wanted his followers to be only the last kind: faithful. Faithful waiters knew God would move. However, they waited *actively*. Paul prayed that God would make him into this kind of follower of Jesus, and not any other.

v. 2

Continue steadfastly in prayer, being watchful in it with thanksgiving.

3 At the same time, pray also for us, that God may open to us a door for the word, to declare the mystery of Christ, on account of which I am in prison– **4** that I may make it clear, which is how I ought to speak.

5 Walk in wisdom toward outsiders, making the best use of the time. **6** Let your speech always be gracious, seasoned with salt, so that you may know how you ought to answer each person.

today is:

I am grateful for:

I am praying for:

SCRIPTURE TO REMEMBER:

observations:

application:

PRAYERFUL RESPONSE:

discussion

We have discussed life in the church and what it looks like when we live in the peace of Christ and knowledge of the gospel. Last time we talked about what it looks like behind the closed doors of our homes. Today we are going to take it a step further. We are leaving the church, leaving our homes, and stepping out into the world. Sound scary? Let's dive in!

In our passage today, Paul is reminding the Colossians what it really means to live out their faith. As servants of Christ, they have been given a ministry. That ministry (or purpose) is revealed in their conversion. Just like the Colossians, we are called to the same ministry. This ministry involves two things: prayer and evangelism.

Prayer

If you were to ask Christians what they wish they would do more in their walk with the Lord, I'm sure "to pray more" would be listed by the majority. I wish I prayed more. It's so easy for life to get busy and to go a whole day without even saying a sentence to God. It's also really easy to have so much and yet thank him so little.

What kind of prayer does Paul exhort the Colossians to? Let's break it down.

1. **"Continue steadfastly"** (ESV), or "devote yourselves" (NASB), from *proskartereō*, "to persevere, wait on (continually)." [1]

2. Be **"watchful"** (ESV), "keeping alert" (NASB), from *grēgoreō*, "to keep awake, be vigilant." [2]

3. **"With thanksgiving"** (ESV), from *eucharistia*, "gratitude." [3]

First, we must be devoted (and persevere) when it comes to our prayers. We must stay "awake" and prayer is a good way to do that. Jesus tells a parable in Luke that hits on this same idea: "Stay dressed for action and keep your lamps burning, and be like men who are waiting for their master to come home from the wedding feast, so that they may open the door to him at once when he comes and knocks. Blessed are those servants whom the master finds awake when he comes. Truly, I say to you, he will dress himself for the service and have them recline at the table, and he will come and serve them. If he comes in the second watch, or in the third, and finds them awake, blessed are those servants! But know this, that if the master of the house had known at what hour the thief was coming, he would not have left his house to be broken into. You also must be ready, for the Son of Man is coming at an hour you do not expect." (Luke 12:35-40)

Secondly, while we are here on this broken earth waiting for our God to return and take us to our rightful home with him, we must stay awake and persevere. Furthermore, we can use the metaphor of sleep being referred to death. Remember, you have been made ALIVE. This is not a life you can get through on autopilot. This is a life where you have to persevere and stay awake, even when your eyes are heavy, even when the temptation is all around. The good news is, we have been given so much grace. Your life is being renewed every day. Tomorrow is a fresh start.

The third point is to let our prayers be done in thanksgiving. This is not a new thought. Paul has been writing about thanksgiving since the very opening of this letter. However, thanksgiving isn't just a little "thanks" notecard when God gives you something. Thanksgiving is a whole lifestyle. It is an act of worship. It is offering everything you have been given—the good and bad—up to God and praising him for it.

Thanksgiving is your sacrifice, especially when it is the humble thanksgiving of suffering. When you say, "God, thank you for the pain. Even though it hurts and doesn't make sense and I really don't like it, you are still good."

It isn't easy. I know that. It took a lot of wrestling with God and my own fears to come to this point. I had to give him total control of my life and that is very scary for someone who likes to plan every last detail.

For a long time, my prayers were self-seeking. They weren't done out of faith, or if they were, it was very small faith. I used to get discouraged by that. However, when I read "...if you have faith like a grain of mustard seed, you will say to this mountain, 'Move from here to there,' and it will move, and nothing will be impossible for you" (Matthew 17:20), I was reminded that even the smallest of faith matters.

My prayers began to change. I followed Paul's instructions. I suddenly found myself praying more and thanking God more. And oh! How my life began to change. I saw things differently. I had joy. I picked up my dream of being an author from the dust and asked God to shape it the way he wanted it to look. I guess it looked something more like this book you're reading right now! Trust me, none of this was my own doing. If I had anything to do with it, I wouldn't have gone anywhere. Everything that has happened, everything that has changed, it is ALL because of Christ. It's because I prayed that Jesus would come BEFORE all things in my life.

It's not like I've made it there yet, and that I don't have days of doubt and fear, because I have a lot of them. But I'm learning that what I'm seeing isn't always the full picture, and often times it takes "looking up" to find your footing again. One of the best ways to do this is to pray. And to keep praying even when you don't want to.

One of the things Paul asks the Colossians to pray for is that God would open a "door for the word" (v. 3). He is asking that they pray for God to lead all of us in the way of evangelism. This is another great mark of leadership. Paul not only began this letter praying for the Colossians, but he asks them to pray for him too. And he is vulnerable with them by telling them what isn't his strong suit: he asks them to pray that God would help him be clear.

Paul wishes to continue proclaiming the gospel, EVEN THOUGH he is in prison for it. My encouragement to those who find evangelism uncomfortable is this: you have nothing to lose and EVERYTHING to gain. Maybe you won't gain anything on this earth. But we are called to fix our eyes on things above, anyway.

Evangelism

In the second half of our passage, Paul gives the Colossians one more task in their new way of living: evangelism. He gives them the steps of WISE evangelism:

1. Make the most of every opportunity (v. 5).
2. Be gracious (v. 6).
3. Present the gospel in an appealing way (v. 6).
4. Speak appropriately to each individual person (v. 6).

In our modern day Christianity, I think we fail to grasp how urgent a matter evangelism is. Just as we must be watchful in prayer because we don't know the day or hour of Christ's return, each person we share the gospel with could be the last one who hears it. Grace freely given is a story that is meant to be shared!

How do you even begin a conversation about Jesus with someone? Are you shuddering? It shouldn't be nerve racking because you have nothing to lose, and everything to gain! We need to be less afraid of what people will think of us if we start talking about Jesus and more concerned with what Jesus can do if we start talking about him!

So, let's begin with grace, because that's where Christ began with us. Be gracious to that person. Don't yell at them on the street corner, don't tell them they are going straight to hell. Meet them where they are. That's grace!

Second, don't make the gospel dull. The story of Jesus and the salvation he offers everyone is far from dull! It is so full of life, so exciting, so unlike anything else in the world that we should be presenting it that way. Paul says to let their speech be "seasoned with salt" in verse 6. Like a chef preparing a gourmet meal, you are presenting it well and making it taste good. How you share the gospel should be so "salty" that it makes their mouths water. Your cry should be something like that of Psalm 34:8:

"Oh, taste and see that the LORD is good!"

Finally, every person that you share the gospel with is different. Everyone learns and connects differently. You have to weigh each person and see what they respond the best to. This takes practice, but DON'T be afraid to start! It also takes a lot of prayer that God would give you the wisdom to share how it is appropriate. Sometimes the best way to start the conversation with someone is by sharing your own story of God's work in you.

Our prayer should be like Paul's when it comes to evangelism: "that God may open to us a door for the word, to declare the mystery of Christ...that [we] may make it clear."

If you want to know exactly what to say to someone you are evangelizing, I would like to recommend the book "Share Jesus Without Fear" by William Fay. It's a pretty quick and easy read and is very helpful. Here are the verses that he gives to walk people through the gospel:

1. Romans 3:23
2. Romans 6:23
3. John 3:3
4. John 14:6
5. Romans 10:9-11
6. 2 Corinthians 5:15
7. Revelation 3:20 [4]

Link these verses together in your bible by noting the references that follow. Give your bible to the person you are evangelizing and have them read these verses aloud. Ask them what each one means to them. Keep asking them until they give you a proper answer. You will find that each verse leads to another and neatly summarizes the gospel! (*In the back of this book, I will include a card that that has these verses, as well as some questions that you can walk through with others. You can cut it out and keep in your bible.)

Here is your encouragement when it comes to the fears that arise when thinking about evangelizing, and you can find it in Matthew 28: "Now the eleven disciples went to Galilee, to the mountain to which Jesus had directed them. And when they saw him they worshiped him, but some doubted. And Jesus came and said to them, 'All authority in heaven and on earth has been given to me. Go therefore and make disciples of all nations, baptizing them in the name of the Father and of the Son and of the Holy Spirit, teaching them to observe all that I have commanded you. And behold, I am with you always, to the end of the age'" (Matthew 28:16-20).

There's a couple things to note here:

1. The disciples went where Jesus directed them.

2. They worshiped him—but some had doubts.

3. Jesus CAME to them and met them where they were, even in their doubt.

4. Jesus has ALL AUTHORITY.

5. Just like the disciples, we are called to make more disciples, baptize, and teach.

6. YOU ARE NOT ALONE.

If you have doubt, fear, anxiety, depression, pain, confusion...worship him. He will COME TO YOU wherever you are and meet you in it. He has called you to go out and make disciples, but you don't need to fear because he is ABOVE ALL THINGS (remember when we talked about this earlier?) and there is NOTHING that can separate you from his love. Whatever fears and lies are holding you back, find your confidence, peace, and comfort in this, my friends. And wherever you are, whatever you're stuck in, Jesus says to you, "behold, I am with you always, to the end of the age."

Discussion Questions

1. What are some practical ways your prayer-life can become more like Paul shows us?

2. What is one thing that is heavy on your heart that you can lift up to God right now?

3. What is the scariest thing about sharing the story of Jesus with others for you?

4. Think about someone you can share the gospel with. What are the steps you can take to evangelize them?

Fulfill the ministry

(Colossians 4:17)

Antioch, 49 A.D.

I would like to visit all the brothers we have witnessed to again and see how they are faring," Paul said as he sat down at the table. Barnabas took a sip from his cup as he propped himself against the back wall.

"I think that's a good idea," he answered. Paul could tell he was hesitant at saying what he was thinking. He raised a crooked eyebrow in curiosity as he tried to imagine what Barnabas was going to say. He was not prepared for what came out of his mouth next.

"I would like to bring Mark with us."

"Mark?" Paul exclaimed, feeling the heat of anger rise to his face. Barnabas put his cup down and straightened up.

"But Barnabas, you know what he did. Mark deserted us in Pamphylia. He has not been faithful to do the work with us," Paul continued, shaking his head. "How can you be so certain he won't do that again? We cannot invest so much in a deserter."

"You know very well that Mark has apologized for that. I want to give him a second chance," Barnabas replied, coming towards the table where Paul was.

Paul rose to his feet and felt the frustration churning within him. He did not trust Mark. He feared being hurt once again and decided it was better to cut him out before that could happen.

"Paul, you must forgive as Christ forgave our sins," Barnabas said.

Paul remained still.

"How can you preach the good news of the gospel when you do not live it out yourself? You must extend your forgiveness to those who don't deserve it. Don't be a hypocrite." Barnabas' words cut sharp into Paul's heart and he knew in that moment that he was losing his friend's company.

"It is clear that we do not see eye-to-eye on this matter. Therefore, I will take Mark with me to Cyprus," Barnabas continued after a long period of silence. Paul felt betrayed, and his heart crumpled within his chest. He watched as Barnabas left the room and met Mark outside.

When Barnabas and Mark sailed out the next day, Paul was defeated. He thought Barnabas would change his mind after a night's sleep, but he didn't. What was worse, he did not even look Paul in the eye as he departed.

"What am I to do next, Lord?" he heard himself praying over and over. "I cannot go on alone."

He felt a tap on his shoulder and turned. There stood Silas.

"I know that I was sent here from Jerusalem with you to bring the council's letter to the Gentile believers here in Antioch," he began. "However I feel as if I should not depart from you and that you need someone to accompany you on your journeys. The Lord is showing me that one man cannot do this life by himself."

Paul smiled a little. "Please come with me. I am leaving for Syria in the morning."

Although Paul was sad to not have Barnabas' company as they set out on their journey, he was very grateful to have Silas with him. God was mending and encouraging his broken heart through this man. And though he did not know it at the time, God would be placing many more people in his path to encourage him all throughout his life. Paul's heart ached for the believers to come together and encourage one another. He pictured the church functioning like a body—Jesus Christ as the head and everyone else with their own role and function working together as the entire body grows in maturity and strength. 1

v. 7-9

Tychicus will tell you all about my activities. He is a beloved brother and faithful minister and fellow servant in the Lord. I have sent him to you for this very purpose, that you may know how we are and that he may encourage your hearts, and with him Onesimus, our faithful and beloved brother, who is one of you. They will tell you of everything that has taken place here.

10 Aristarchus my fellow prisoner greets you, and Mark the cousin of Barnabas (concerning whom you have received instructions—if he comes to you, welcome him), **11** and Jesus who is called Justus. These are the only men of the circumcision among my fellow workers for the kingdom of God, and they have been a comfort to me. **12** Epaphras, who is one of you, a servant of Christ Jesus, greets you, always struggling on your behalf in his prayers, that you may stand mature and fully assured in all the will of God. **13** For I bear him witness that he has worked hard for you and for those in Laodicea and in Hierapolis. **14** Luke the beloved physician greets you, as does Demas. **15** Give my greetings to the brothers at Laodicea, and to Nympha and the church in her house. **16** And when this letter has been read among you, have it also read in the church of the Laodiceans; and see that you also read the letter from Laodicea. **17** And say to Archippus, "See that you fulfill the ministry that you have received in the Lord."

18 I, Paul, write this greeting with my own hand. Remember my chains. Grace be with you.

today is:

I am grateful for:

I am praying for:

SCRIPTURE TO REMEMBER:

observations:

application:

PRAYERFUL RESPONSE:

discussion

There's A LOT of names in our passage today, right? I don't know about you, but this is a passage that I would often skim over. You may even be wondering why God inspired this part to be in His Word. However, I'm going to challenge you to NOT skim. If you did, that's ok—we'll dig a little deeper into the meaning of this passage together.

This passage shows us that if we are Christians, we are on a team (the body of Christ) that is devoted to serving Christ together. It is clear that Paul was not a solo act because in such a short book where only a verse is devoted to wives, husbands, children, sin (etc) each, Paul takes the remaining twelve verses to commend his fellow workers in Christ.

7 Things We Can Learn About the Church

1. It is a team.
2. It is made up of men and women from different racial and socioeconomic backgrounds.
3. It is the family of God.
4. Every member is a voluntary servant/slave of Christ
5. It is focused on prayer and the Word with the purpose of helping each member stand mature in Christ.
6. It has members who often disappoint us.
7. It thrives in an atmosphere where every member is encouraged to become all that God wants them to be.

Paul reminds the Colossians of the purpose of his letter in verses eight and twelve: that they may know how Paul and his team are doing, that they may be encouraged, and that they may "stand mature and fully assured in all the will of God." He writes personal encouragements to each member of his team, except Demas. We learn later that Demas deserts Paul (2 Timothy 4:10). Although it is sad and obviously discouraging when people disappoint us, there is encouragement and hope found in the story of Mark, the cousin of Barnabas.

During Paul's first missionary journey with Barnabas, Mark deserted them (Acts 13:13). When Barnabas tried to convince Paul to give Mark a second chance, it lead to a rift between them (Acts 15:36-41). But here, twelve years later, Paul is telling the Colossians to accept Mark if he comes to them without reservation.

While Demas warns us of the possibility of abandonment, Mark encourages us with the hope of restoration when we have failed. What's even more encouraging about Mark is God used him to write one of the gospels in the New Testament! God uses the unlikely everyday!

This passage is a reminder that we all need encouragement in this journey. And we all need to remember that we aren't doing this alone. Even if people disappoint us, God never deserts us.

Paul encourages all his fellow workers or slaves of Christ. He has a special encouragement for Epaphras and his devotion to the church in Colossae. Paul says that he "struggling" on their behalf in his prayers. We talked about the importance of prayer last time, and this only builds off of that.

Here we see that prayer is not easy. The word "struggling" (ESV), or "laboring earnestly" (NASB) comes from the Greek *agonidzo*, or agony 2. Paul writes of Epaphras' "deep concern" for the Colossians in a way that was used to describe the pain of struggling in battle.

Your prayers are fighting a battle, and it is often a battle that we do not see or even realize is there. But prayer is so important and powerful! Not only are we Christ's servants, but we are his soldiers—an army preparing for battle. This is why encouragement is CRUCIAL to the health of the Church. But we have hope because we know that Jesus Christ has ALREADY WON the battle. However, we don't stop fighting until he returns to take us home.

Soldier, God has called you to put on your armor. He has called you to "stand mature and fully assured in all the will of God" (4:12). What is the will of God? Paul doesn't mean discovering your career. The will of God is how God wants us to live—and he shows us what that looks like in his Word. We learned that back in 1:9 and 3:16. We've seen it all throughout the book of Colossians!

In Colossians, Paul shows us that God is seeking to restore our posture toward three things:

1. Our relationship with him, which is reconciled through faith in Jesus (1:1-3:4)
2. Our relationships with each other as we walk in love (3:5-4:1, 7-18)
3. Our relationship with those who do not know Christ, through prayer and wise witness (4:2-6)

This is the will of God. This is your ministry. Just as Paul encouraged Archippus, so I encourage you:

"See that you fulfill the ministry that you have received in the Lord." (4:17)

This is not something that you choose. It's something you have received in the Lord. It is a lifestyle. Epaphras' prayer for the Colossians is certainly the same for all Christians. To "stand mature" (or "perfect," as we see in 3:14) means to put on the new self, to live a life that is "bearing fruit and increasing" (1:6) through the power of the Holy Spirit, and—as we see in Paul's encouragement to those in this passage—to be a faithful servant.

And the power of grace is that we can find encouragement in the fact that if we continue to do all these things (and even when we fail), one beautiful day we will gain an inheritance (because we are slaves AND children) with the greatest affirmation of all: "Well done, good and faithful servant" (Matthew 25:23).

In the meantime, let's live in a way that puts Christ before all things. Grace be with you.

Discussion Questions

1. What are some signs of a healthy church?

2. Is there such a thing as the "right" church for you?

3. How can you contribute to a church?

4. How can you encourage others in a church?

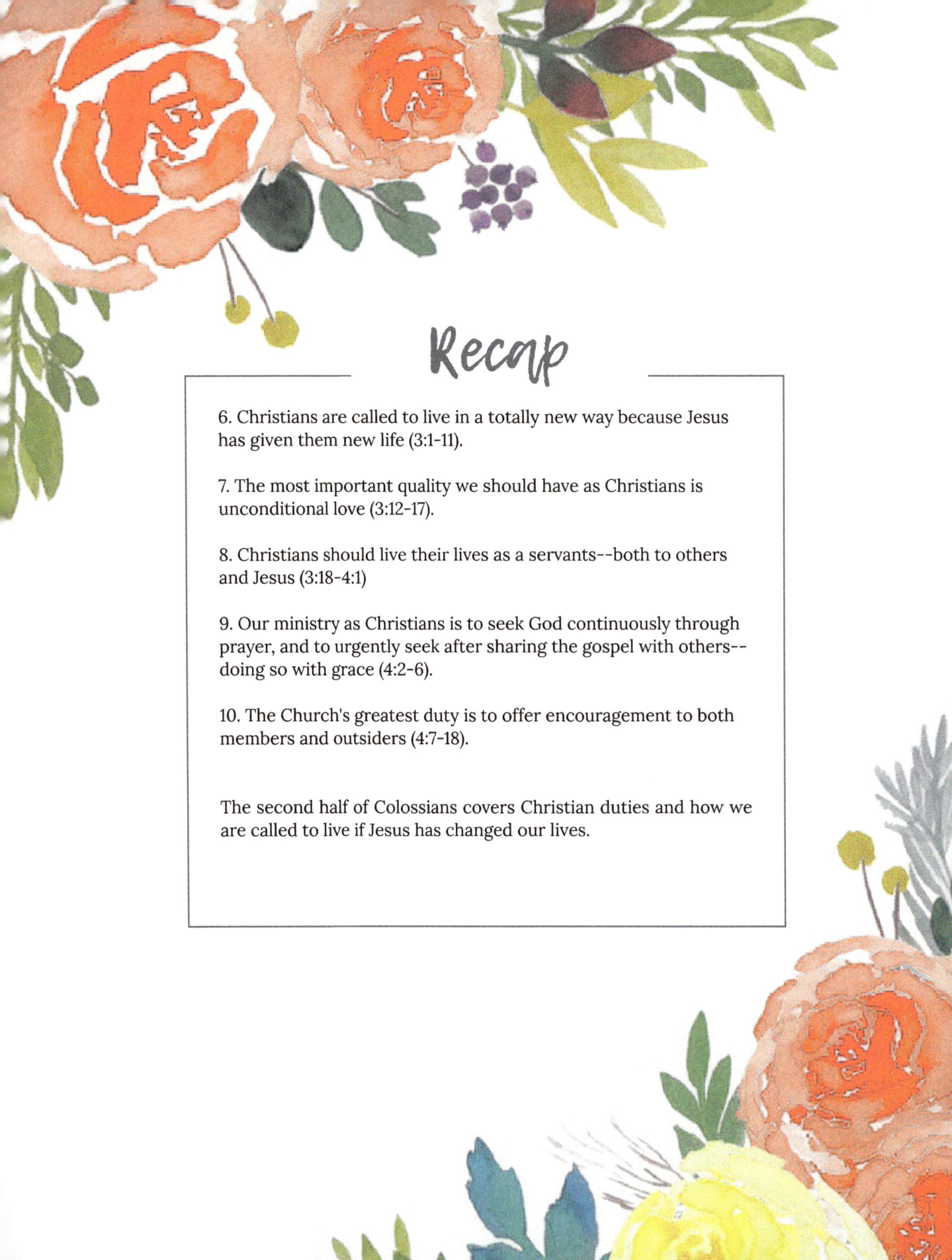

Recap

6. Christians are called to live in a totally new way because Jesus has given them new life (3:1-11).

7. The most important quality we should have as Christians is unconditional love (3:12-17).

8. Christians should live their lives as a servants--both to others and Jesus (3:18-4:1)

9. Our ministry as Christians is to seek God continuously through prayer, and to urgently seek after sharing the gospel with others-- doing so with grace (4:2-6).

10. The Church's greatest duty is to offer encouragement to both members and outsiders (4:7-18).

The second half of Colossians covers Christian duties and how we are called to live if Jesus has changed our lives.

You can cut this page out and place it in a 8x10 frame to display wherever you need the reminder.

"IF THEN YOU HAVE BEEN RAISED WITH CHRIST, SEEK THE THINGS THAT ARE ABOVE, WHERE CHRIST IS, SEATED AT THE RIGHT HAND OF GOD ."

COLOSSIANS 3:1

Final Thoughts

God has given us new life, and with that comes an *entirely* new identity. This radically changes our outlook, but oh how easy this is to forget.

I don't know what you're daily struggle is. I don't know what brings you joy and what makes you cry. What makes you strong or weak. But I do know that you have a story and you have "something" for all of these things.

I wrote this book not only to learn some things myself, but to encourage others. Colossians spoke truth into my life when I was at one of my weakest points. It is may prayer that God uses his Word to do the same in yours.

No matter what you're facing--if it's any consolation--you are not alone in it. But more importantly, God is BIGGER than it. Constantly, I let fear tell me that whatever I am facing is too big to handle. While it may be too big for me, God is bigger, and he goes before it.

I titled this book "Before All Things" because one of the biggest themes in the book of Colossians is that Jesus is where we find life. I wanted this to be one of the main "themes" of my own life, and I began praying that God would help me put Jesus before all the things in my life. Thus, the title of this book was born!

If you live in fear--Jesus is before it. If you live in pain--Jesus is before it. No matter what you face, no matter who you are, Jesus has made a way for all of us to be courageous! I want to share part of a prayerful journal entry that I wrote to God before I embarked on the journey of writing this book:

I have been asking why a lot lately. Why this pain? Why do I feel like this? Why can't it be different? It's funny how the answer has been there all along, it just took a little more ice-picking to break through...

"Be strong and very courageous" (Joshua 1:9) has been my motto for as long as I can remember. God told this to all the leaders he was building up in the Old Testament, and he said it to Paul too. He's been telling me this. But recently he's been telling me more.

This is what he told me: "even the fearful and the doubters can find courage when they spend time with Jesus." Look at Thomas in John 11:18. Look at Peter when he follows Jesus onto the water. Look at David. There are so many examples.

I'm fearful and doubting. Jesus meets me HERE. And he reminds me of my hope. That is how I can find courage. I know he is with me even in my pain and suffering. Here (in him) is where I can stand courageous once again. And the first step is to see Jesus as he is and where he belongs: before all things.

Notes

CHAPTER 1:
    1. Inspired by Col. 1:7; 4:12
    2. James Strong, *Strong's Expanded Exhaustive Concordance of the Bible* (Nashville: Thomas Nelson, 2009), s.v. "laid up."
    3. Strong, *Strong's Expanded Exhaustive Concordance of the Bible*, s.v. "gospel."

CHAPTER 2:
    1. Inspired by Acts 13:13-49
    2. Robert Atkin, "Christ, Creation and the Church in the Colossian Hymn (Colossians 1:15 20)," Robert K. Atkin, October 18, 2017, accessed April 21, 2018, http://robertatkin.net/essays/christ-creation-church-colossian-hymn colossians-115-20/.

CHAPTER 3:
    1. Inspired by Acts 7:54-50;14:19
    2. George Eldon Ladd, T*he Gospel of the Kingdom: Scriptural Studies in the Kingdom of God.* (Wm. B. Eerdmans Publishing, 1959).
    3. Strong, s.v. "rejoice."
    4. Strong, s.v. "stewardship."

CHAPTER 4:
    1. Inspired by Acts 9:1-15
    2. Strong, s.v. "received."
    3. Strong, s.v. "so walk."
    4. Strong, s.v. "rooted."
    5. Strong, s.v. "built up."
    6. Strong, s.v. "established."
    7. Strong, s.v. "filled."

CHAPTER 5:
    1. Strong, s.v. "shadow."
    2. Strong, s.v. "substance."

CHAPTER 6:
  1. Inspired by Acts 9:26-28

CHAPTER 7:
  1. Inspired by Acts 11:25-30
  2. Strong, s.v. "chosen."

CHAPTER 8:
  1. Inspired by Acts 28:30-31; Philemon 1:12-16
  2. Aristotle, *Politics 1.5*.
  3. Strong, s.v. "obey."
  4. Strong, s.v. "by the way of eye-service."
  5. Strong, s.v. "people pleasers."
  6. Strong, s.v. "sincerity."
  7. Strong, s.v. "fearing."
  8. Strong, s.v. "heartily."

CHAPTER 9:
  1. Strong, s.v. "continue steadfastly."
  2. Strong, s.v. "be watchful."
  3. Strong, s.v. "with thanksgiving."
  4. William Fay and Linda E. Shepherd, *Share Jesus Without Fear* (Nashville, TN: Broadman & Holman Publishers, 1999).

CHAPTER 10:
  1. Inspired by Acts 15:36-41
  2. Strong, s.v. "struggling.

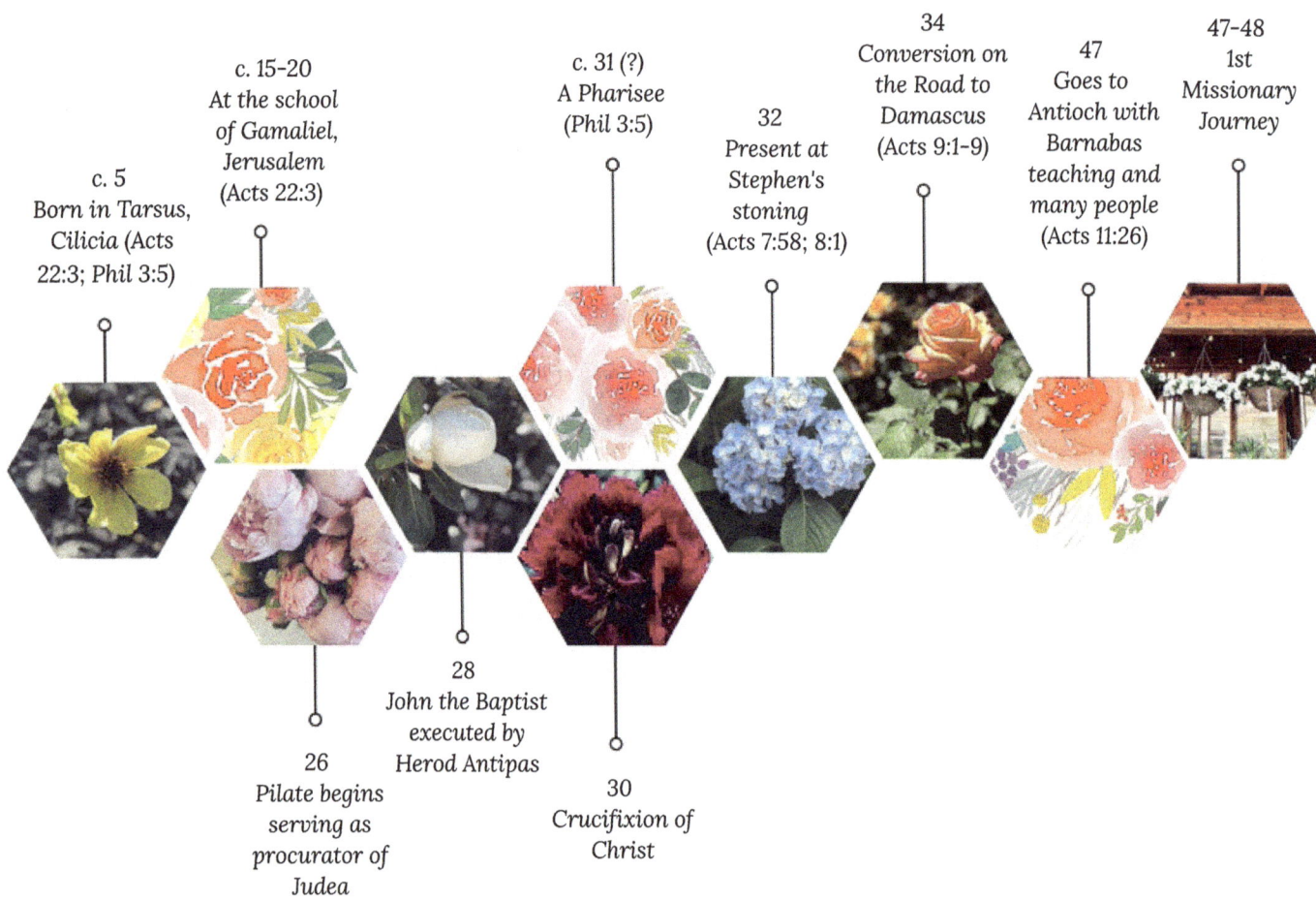

c. 5
Born in Tarsus,
Cilicia (Acts
22:3; Phil 3:5)

c. 15–20
At the school
of Gamaliel,
Jerusalem
(Acts 22:3)

26
Pilate begins
serving as
procurator of
Judea

28
John the Baptist
executed by
Herod Antipas

30
Crucifixion of
Christ

c. 31 (?)
A Pharisee
(Phil 3:5)

32
Present at
Stephen's
stoning
(Acts 7:58; 8:1)

34
Conversion on
the Road to
Damascus
(Acts 9:1-9)

47
Goes to
Antioch with
Barnabas
teaching and
many people
(Acts 11:26)

47–48
1st
Missionary
Journey

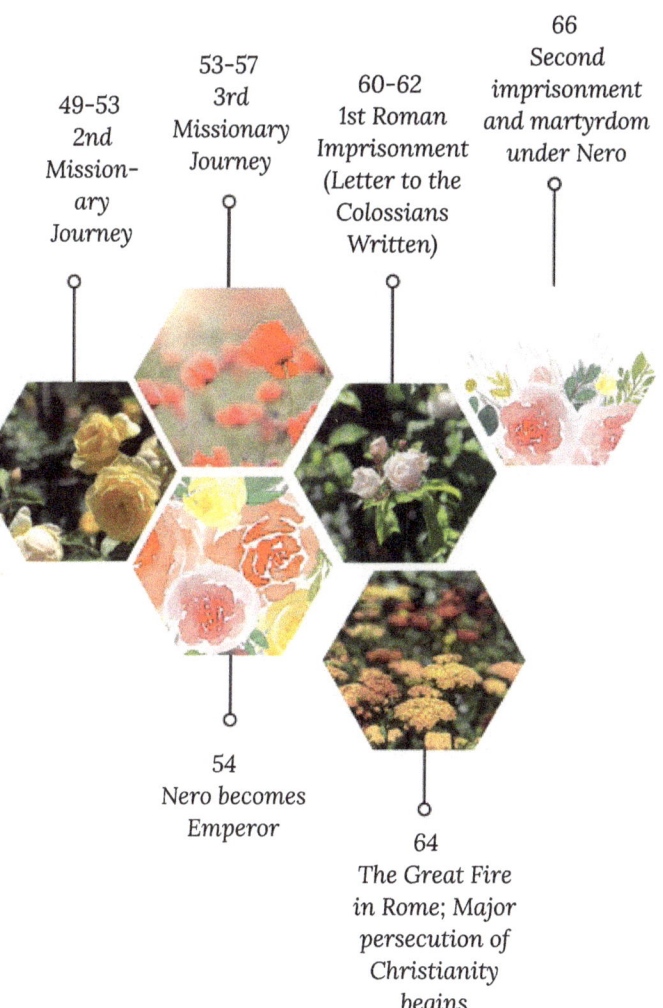

49-53
2nd
Mission-
ary
Journey

53-57
3rd
Missionary
Journey

60-62
1st Roman
Imprisonment
(Letter to the
Colossians
Written)

66
Second
imprisonment
and martyrdom
under Nero

54
Nero becomes
Emperor

64
The Great Fire
in Rome; Major
persecution of
Christianity
begins

"I have fought the good fight, I have finished the race, I have kept the faith." (2 Timothy 4:7)

These were some of Paul's final words to his loved ones before he died, a martyr at the hand of Nero in 66 A.D.

After he met Jesus on the road to Damascus, Paul lived his life in a way that can only be described as faithful.

Paul wrote to the Colossians to encourage them to live spiritually mature lives and to fortify their faith against false-teaching. His letter is a reminder for all of us to strive to live our lives with our eyes set on Jesus. Through the powerful working of the Holy Spirit, we will be strengthened to endure the times of suffering, and we have the hope of glory in Christ waiting for us at the end of the "race."

Spiritual maturity looks less like something we do, and more like Christ coming before all things.

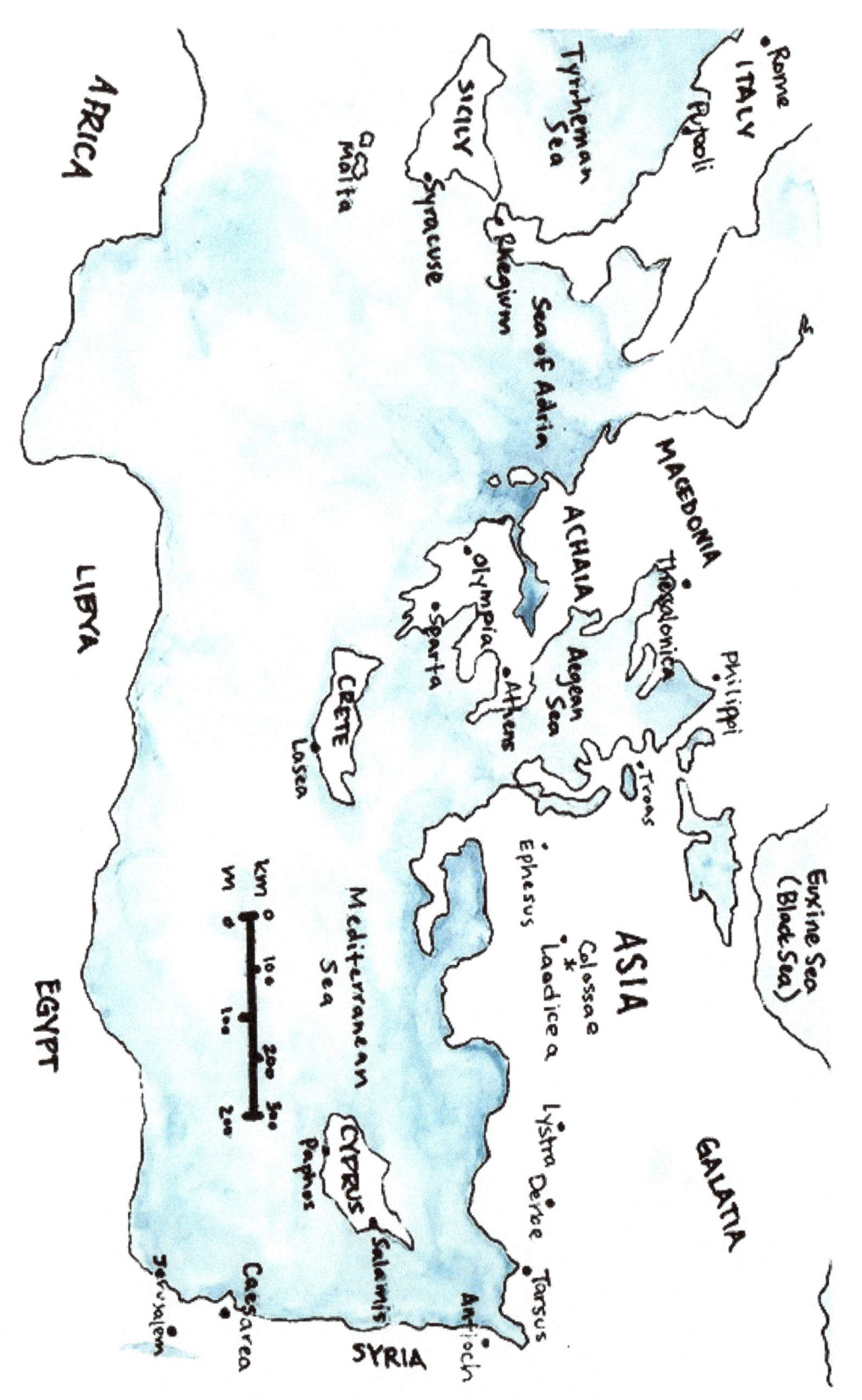

You can cut this page out and place the cards wherever you need the reminder.

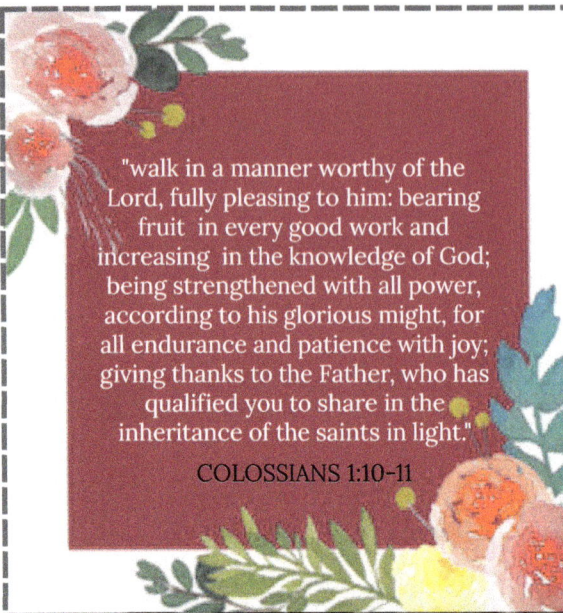

"walk in a manner worthy of the Lord, fully pleasing to him: bearing fruit in every good work and increasing in the knowledge of God; being strengthened with all power, according to his glorious might, for all endurance and patience with joy; giving thanks to the Father, who has qualified you to share in the inheritance of the saints in light."

COLOSSIANS 1:10-11

"continue in the faith, stable and steadfast, not shifting from the hope of the gospel that you heard, which has been proclaimed in all creation under heaven, and of which I, Paul, became a minister."

Colossians 1:23

"Him we proclaim, warning everyone and teaching everyone with all wisdom, that we may present everyone mature in Christ."

COLOSSIANS 1:28

"THEREFORE, AS YOU RECEIVED CHRIST JESUS THE LORD, SO WALK IN HIM, ROOTED AND BUILT UP IN HIM AND ESTABLISHED IN THE FAITH, JUST AS YOU WERE TAUGHT, ABOUNDING IN THANKSGIVING."

colossians 2:6-7

"AND YOU, WHO WERE DEAD IN YOUR TRESPASSES AND THE UNCIRCUMCISION OF YOUR FLESH, GOD MADE ALIVE TOGETHER WITH HIM, HAVING FORGIVEN US ALL OUR TRESPASSES, BY CANCELING THE RECORD OF DEBT THAT STOOD AGAINST US WITH ITS LEGAL DEMANDS. THIS HE SET ASIDE, NAILING IT TO THE CROSS."

Colossians 2:13,14

"These are a shadow of the things to come, but the substance belongs to Christ."

COLOSSIANS 2:17

You can cut this page out and place the cards wherever you need the reminder.

"IF THEN YOU HAVE BEEN RAISED WITH CHRIST, SEEK THE THINGS THAT ARE ABOVE, WHERE CHRIST IS, SEATED AT THE RIGHT HAND OF GOD."

COLOSSIANS 3:1

"Put on the new self, which is being renewed in knowledge after the image of its creator."

Colossians 3:10

"PUT ON THEN, AS GOD'S CHOSEN ONES, HOLY AND BELOVED, COMPASSIONATE HEARTS, KINDNESS, HUMILITY, MEEKNESS, AND PATIENCE, BEARING WITH ONE ANOTHER AND, IF ONE HAS A COMPLAINT AGAINST ANOTHER, FORGIVING EACH OTHER; AS THE LORD HAS FORGIVEN YOU, SO YOU ALSO MUST FORGIVE. AND ABOVE ALL THESE PUT ON LOVE, WHICH BINDS EVERYTHING TOGETHER IN PERFECT HARMONY."

colossians 3:12-14

"Whatever you do, work heartily, as for the Lord and not for men, knowing that from the Lord you will receive the inheritance as your reward. You are serving the Lord Christ."

COLOSSIANS 3:23-24

"At the same time, pray also for us, that God may open to us a door for the word, to declare the mystery of Christ, on account of which I am in prison."

Colossians 4:3

"See that you fulfill the ministry that you have received in the Lord."

COLOSSIANS 4:17

You can cut this page out and place the cards wherever you need the reminder.

QUESTIONS FOR STUDYING THE BIBLE

OBSERVE

- Who was this written to?
- What is happening in the passage?
- When and where did this take place?
- Why did the author write this?

INTERPRET

- What would the original hearers have thought?
- How does this fit in with the greater narrative of the bible?
- Are there other parts of scripture that come to mind when reading this?

With these in mind...

APPLY

- What does this tell you about who God is?
- What does this tell you about your sin and need for a Savior?
- How might these truths transform your everyday?

pray.

"SHARE JESUS WITHOUT FEAR"
adapted from the book by William Fay

The Five Share Jesus Questions:

1. Do you have any kind of spiritual belief?
2. To you, who is Jesus?
3. Do you think there is a heaven or a hell?
4. If you died tonight, where would you go? If heaven, why?
5. If what you were believing were not true, would you want to know?

The Share Jesus Scriptures:

1. Romans 3:23
2. Romans 6:23
3. John 3:3
4. John 14:6
5. Romans 10:9-11
6. 2 Corinthians 5:15
7. Revelation 3:20

The Five Commitment Questions:

1. Are you a sinner?
2. Do you want forgiveness of your sins?
3. Do you believe Jesus Christ died on the cross for you and rose again?
4. Are you willing to surrender your life to Jesus Christ?
5. Are you ready to invite Jesus Christ into your life and into your heart?

The Sinner's Prayer

"Heavenly Father, I have sinned against you. I want forgiveness for all my sins. I believe that Jesus died on the cross for me and rose again. Father, I give you my life to do with as you wish. I want Jesus Christ to come into my life and into my heart. This I ask in Jesus' name. Amen"

Paper patterns for bookmarks (see next pg. for instructions)

Page Corner Bookmark

1. Make initial diagonal folds (pattern side down)
2. Fold in corners to meet in the center
3. Fold in half along diagonal crease
4. Bring the corners up to meet in a diamond shape
5. Tuck the flaps in the inside pocket
6. Ready to put on your book page corner!

Thanks

To my husband, Chris, for encouraging me to pursue my dreams and grow in my relationship with the Lord. This book would never have even started without you.

To my parents for raising a dreamer and setting examples of what it looks like to be a faithful servant of God.

To my grandparents, who invested just as much time into studying Colossians as me, and for encouraging me with truth along the way.

To my aunt and uncle for giving me the journaling bible that started it all.

To God for providing for every need while I embark on this crazy journey. All the glory belongs to him and him alone!

A little about the author

Prestyn Kylie Cotuna lives in Portland, Oregon with her loving husband, Chris (yes, the very one below) and a wide array of houseplants. When she's not spending time with her loved ones, you can find her making some kind of art, taking pictures, or singing. Prestyn first fell in love with writing and illustrating "books" when she was eight years old. Then, she fell in love with something even better a little over a decade later: studying God's Word. She left a Creative Writing program in Oregon to pursue a degree in Biblical Studies at Briercrest Bible College in the Canadian prairies. It was there that God arrested her heart and filled it with an inherent need for spending time with him. She knows what it's like to not like reading the Bible, but she also knows what it's like to not be able to get enough of it. *Before All Things* was borne out of a desire to help others fall in love with the richness of God's Word and the tremendous impact it has on our everyday lives. You can connect with her on her social media or her website: www.prestynkyliecotuna.com.

@prestynkyliecotuna

Christian Cotuna is married to his beautiful wife, Prestyn. He enjoys longboarding and taking pictures (sometimes at the same time) and making killer sandwiches. When Chris first met Prestyn she was passionately studying and writing about the book of Colossians. He sent her an email encouraging her to never stop pursuing Christ and sharing about the wonders of His Word. Little did he know that just over a year later, he would be married to that girl he madly fell in love with, and helping her turn a dream of writing about God's Word into reality. For many years Chris has had a passion for following Christ, and he especially loves doing so by ministering to people through healthcare. He is currently pursuing his doctorate with the desire to continue using this setting to care for others physically, mentally, and spiritually.

Lightning Source UK Ltd.
Milton Keynes UK
UKHW050025230119
335986UK00001B/18/P

9 780464 760733